all author profits and a percentage of the publisher's
profits go to the Magic Sandwich Project –
a registered charity

change activist

THE

TO DO IT —

ONLY WAY
IS TO DO IT

change activist

make big things happen fast

Carmel McConnell

www.yourmomentum.com
the stuff that drives you

What is momentum?

Momentum is for people who want to make things happen in their career and their life, who want to work at something they enjoy and that's worthy of their talent and their time. Momentum people have values and principles and question who they are, what they do, and who for. Wherever they work, they want to feel proud of what they do. And they are hungry for information, stimulation, ideas and answers. ...

Momentum online

Visit *www.yourmomentum.com* to be part of the talent community. Here you'll find a full listing of current and future books, an archive of articles by momentum authors, sample chapters and self-assessment tools. While you're there, post your work/life questions to our momentum coaches and sign up to receive free newsletters with even more stuff to drive you.

PEARSON EDUCATION LIMITED

Head Office:
Edinburgh Gate
Harlow CM20 2JE
Tel: +44 (0)1279 623623
Fax: +44 (0)1279 431059

London Office:
128 Long Acre, London WC2E 9AN
Tel: +44 (0)20 7447 2000
Fax: +44 (0)20 7447 2170
Website: www.business-minds.com
www.yourmomentum.com

First published in Great Britain in 2001
This edition published in Great Britain in 2003
© Pearson Education Limited 2003

The right of Carmel McConnell to be identified
as Author of this Work has been asserted by
her in accordance with the Copyright, Designs
and Patents Act 1988.

ISBN 1 843 04027 1

British Library Cataloguing in Publication Data
A CIP catalogue record for this book can be
obtained from the British Library

10 9 8 7 6 5 4 3 2 1

Design by Claire Brodmann Book Designs,
Lichfield, Staffs
Typeset by Northern Phototypesetting Co. Ltd,
Bolton
Printed and bound in Great Britain by
Bookcraft, Midsomer Norton

The Publishers' policy is to use paper
manufactured from sustainable forests.

thank you ...

to all the people who helped me worry less and trust more. Who helped me understand that we can all improve our lives by taking action, however small.

to Gerald McConnell and Patricia Donaghey my parents, checking in from heaven

to my partner Catherine for endless loving support and intellectual challenge

to Carolyn McConnell my sister, the most optimistic activist I know

to Mick Cope for kick-starting my writing career, and for his astonishing day to day generosity and wisdom

to Rachael Anderson for being the kindest, smartest editor a writer could ever have, and for creating her own activist path in publishing (read *Get Ahead and Give a Damn*, published 2003)

to Richard Stagg at Pearson Education for spot-on advice and perspective

to Dave and Heather for generously sharing their home in Fowey

to the late and loved Dennis and Sylvia Rosen, lifelong heroes

to Laura Nickerson, who created a peaceful anti-nuclear campaign in 17 countries

to Wendy Briner, friend and mentor who patiently taught me how to learn

to Craig Leslie and the team at the Great American Bagel Factory for supporting the Magic Sandwich pilot schools in Hackney

to Eileen and Bernard Collins for all that early encouragement

to Wendy, Karen, Olu, Marion and all on the Magic Outcomes team, creating a social leadership programme, with all profits to primary schools

and with love to all the inspiring change activists who keep going and keep laughing.

thank you

contents

chapter 3

practical activism – here's how   93

chapter 4

loyal to your firm, what about you? 171

chapter 5
activism and peaceful dissent   231

about the author

Carmel McConnell has spent her whole life being an activist, firstly at the Greenham Common nuclear missile base and latterly as a global corporate consultant.

Her experiences are testament to the fact that you can think big, have a stake in the decision-making process, turn profits and still have principles.

She now works as a consultant, change activist and author. Carmel's major interest is in the link between social justice and big business, and helping large organizations to learn and apply greater social responsibility in the belief that consumer trust is the ultimate market advantage.

Carmel is donating all her royalties from this book to *The Magic Sandwich Project* – a child poverty charity she set up in 2000 to get nutritious food into schools where malnutrition and under-achievement go hand-in-hand.

A percentage of the publisher's profits also go to this cause.

01

change anyone

how can you take charge of your life?

MANAGING CHANGE, valuing change, embracing change. A constant mantra and yet, according to all the evidence, change management right now simply doesn't work. It doesn't work and that isn't going to change.

Despite megabucks and big brains working flat out, the market remains resolutely out of sync with your company. Or should that be the other way round? Your **Human traffic jams are** employees still don't behave like **starting to form on the** high-performing teams for the **roads out of boring,** customer. Despite the in-house **dehumanizing work** propaganda machine telling them 'how to' at maximum 'colour photo of the boss being sociable' spin capacity.

And you still don't like the way your job makes you feel. Even though you got promoted.

Downshifting portfolio workers apart, we all yearn for a bit more from the career thing. A bit more what, though? Dilbert was funny but a bit sad. The messiahs of positive thinking might be useful, but who can cheerfully attempt a complete lifestyle turnaround, faced with the daily in-tray and a large (let's not think about life, just get through this morning) latte for me please?

There has to be some better way. There is a better way. A principle called change activism. Which goes like this.

Change activism is about taking control at a personal level. This book shows how to apply activist principles to your working life so that you can become more successful. It will help you take action, so you can change your mindset to a more positive, pro-active state. And believe me, that feels so much better and gets much better results than fear.

Change activism turns up the volume on things you care about. Imagine your workplace filled with trust, getting a daily buzz doing something you really care about. Activists have a passionate connection to what needs to be done and a huge sense of fulfilment because that's what happens when your work involves true contribution from the heart. As this book will show, your fulfilment level is directly linked to your contribution level, in whatever occupation.

Change activism also has business benefits. Since the first edition of this book in 2000 the concept of trust as competitive advantage has gone from nice dream to mainstream. Business leaders have to ably demonstrate their trustworthiness in front of their audience of nervous investors, employees and customers. At board level the chain has never been under more market scrutiny. You run your business honestly. You hire honest accountants. You communicate openly because you have nothing to hide. The press trust you. Your employees trust you. Your customers trust your employees. And the business keeps its good reputation. Call it transparency, governance, accountability, stakeholder engagement – it is all about trust.

In this worldwide webbed marketplace, fickle consumer hunger means you have one true source of competitive advantage. The answer to 'can I trust you or not?'. Put yourself

Could you use some change activism in your life?

in the position of a customer now. Or an investor. Or (I hope this feels easier) an employee with choices. Do you trust the promises made where you work? Or does the latest senior message just make you smile, in an amused, gently cynical way? What does the trustometer say where you work?

As a social activist and business practitioner I can show you activist tools that can improve your trust making abilities, challenge your business assumptions and help your profit levels. How? I can encourage your activist self (the optimistic, passionate voice of change in your head) to enhance your 'beyond the bottom line' contribution to the world.

I won't go on about corporate accounting scandals, you've been there and sold the T-shirt. Probably at a loss.

Profit, competitive advantage and employees who stay are proving hard to find in the new economy. Big corporates have to decide on a new way of working. Management for profit by fear? Management for profit by authenticity?

Employees seek fulfilling work and some balance in their lives. Consumers prompt a growth in ethical brands and fair partnerships. Business turns to the uncharted shores of www.anywhere for inspiration. Change is constant and frantic and who knows how best to navigate?

There are still no grown-ups when it comes to handling business change. We tend to stay in our comfort zone, look around, want to ask for approval every ten minutes and take baby steps towards a better place. If we provide a product or service, we hope our customers will applaud, stay loyal, buy more. If we manage, we hope our good employees will stay a while and are fulfilled while giving 100 per cent. These are not unrealistic hopes. But how can you make the changes you want to make?

Here's how. Action is still the only way to make things happen. I believe that our firms will benefit as we change our mindset about our work and our lives and become more powerful, more effective as individuals. More profitable. Promise! So instead of passive, I'm going to push for Big Time Change Activism. Because we need it. Nowhere more than in the world of business. So let's start there.

Our financial systems have been on greed autopilot for too long, a global securities takeover built on **Make more than profit** short-term corporate performance for short-term yields. And now the great investment mirage that has held us, rapt, for years, has finally come to an end.

A number of business leaders have let the moral blueprint slip from their chubby fingers. And even more are strangely silent on the subject of corporate malfeasance, over-stated profits and the shares they sold six months before the journalists found out. Not good enough – not from the perspective of the employee, the shareholder, the consumer or the stakeholder. Isn't it time for a generation of change activist business leaders to create some sleaze-free profit?

Isn't it time for you and I to go into this career thing with eyes open and achieve more than survival year to year? For most people in the world it would be, like, really helpful if someone, somewhere seemed to give a damn about corporate impact on our world, our societies, our air and water supplies. How do you feel?

It's true that some ethics-first business strategies are emerging. There is a change in the air. Consumers expect more. The drinks with chemical additives aren't so cool anymore. Witness Monsanto, Shell, Barclays, Nike. Generic brands are forced to find the bespoke and personal sale. My IBM. My bespoke Calvin Kleins. My tailored *FT* news page. The Internet causing far too many banks to chase far too little business – forcing them to offer a more personalized service. If you saw the film *Minority Report*, with Tom Cruise, the Fox/Dreamwork future was full of this – your virtual assistant checks your iris and asks 'are you here for another pair of those boot cut chinos sir?'. The oversupply of services means businesses have to listen more acutely than ever before.

We can choose to be more morally vocal because as investors, consumers, employees, suppliers (stakeholders for short) we have new powers and with those powers, confidence to assert a wider agenda. Why? Simply demand and supply. Fifty years ago if you had a car to sell you could sell it. The goods weren't there to buy. Twenty years ago the car had to have superior features. Now it has to have superior features, convey a superior lifestyle brand and be almost entirely bespokable. There is a higher asking price for a place in front of the buyer. So companies are striving for the elusive value add. Seeking out pastures new in customized, premium, global. Is there something else I can do for you madam? Would you like the zero emissions option and we'll plant ten trees for every car purchased in October?

It did not always matter: the evolution of trade

Timeframe	What happened
1950s manufacturing focus (economies of scale, production efficiency)	
1960s sales focus (you've never had it so good era)	Chronic
1970s cost focus (oil crisis, recession and rise of Asia Pacific trade)	shortage over time
1980s marketing focus (product proliferation, branding)	becomes
1990s customer focus (Building bespoke relationships)	chronic
Early 21st-century enlightened focus (greater stakeholder inclusion, ethics part of brand package)	oversupply

with thanks to Jane Walker

The good news is that if Gucci say individual customization is the new black, it is one more step away from faceless, luckless consumerism. I've used up all the time I ever want to spend this lifetime on the customer service line, not enjoying the *Four Seasons*, still fourth in the queue waiting for a new phone line, car insurance, locksmith, whatever. We consumers can call more of the shots and we want to feel good about our purchases. And just as we don't invite drug dealers into our homes, we won't visit the megastore/click the website/buy the shares/send the CV to a morally bankrupt business. We'll pay for a sexy new thing with our salaries (i.e. our time, brain, effort), but not with our souls.

Change activism is about developing active moral muscle, which is a pretty useful thing in a time when, let's face it, many of our business leaders have been morally underperforming. Not naming names, Enron, WorldCom, Andersen, Xerox, Global Crossing and that one you read about recently (there's bound to be one) are financially disreputable organizations, despite the nice brand adverts, neatly arranged MBA certificates and gleaming HQs. Now this is not to say business leaders are infected with 'Enronitis' – my belief and experience has been that most are honest, hard-working people. However, there is huge management pressure to perform to target, now, or make way for someone who can, creating a fallible, greed-prone approach at the heart of short-term financial accounting.

Now if that just meant share falls it would be one thing, but it also resulted in a very nasty surprise for employees, subscribed to 'the financial strategy'. We always hoped the highly paid ones knew what they were talking about, and who feels able to question the numbers when they gave you a nice car? It's hard. It is also frowned upon. I don't remember a 'practical whistle-blowing' module in my management studies. The big company tradition of 'have financial information versus have nots' is one good reason to take stock of your working environment. Is it morally barren or lush? For example, is it the norm at your place of work to laugh over the boss's cheeky ways with the budget and thank goodness the customer doesn't know. Or do you try to understand how those figures are created and make a loud noise at the first sign of fiction? What can you do as one person to improve potential weaknesses of conscience within your organization? I believe loads. Imagine how those 200 WorldCom employees got through the day after $3.4 billion was found to have been 'misrepresented' by the previously inspiring set of directors.

During my time as a line manager the numbers were a) boring, b) not what I went to work for, and c) not something I had time to look at in any long day. But if someone had said, try to understand this because financial reports can indicate if this is a decently run organization, I might have been more interested. So right now, please listen. Here I am, saying the numbers are worth some of your energy and attention. Understand how the money moves; is it through a maze of offshore tax vehicles or from straightforward transactions into clear profit, loss and hello Mr Taxman figures? Maybe you already do understand. Great – do your colleagues? Come on in (says the financial director), today I want you to take a look at how we on the board put these numbers together, and then in groups of ten, get your views on how honest we're being. Coffee and ethical interrogation of the board? Does it happen where you are? Would you go along if that invite appeared in your inbox? Would you suggest it?

Believe me, you need a very active sense of moral judgement when it comes to business. *Change Activist* can help you assess the danger of being onboard the newest Enron, before your career and your pension become the last thing on their mind – publicly.

[It's time for] 'a new ethic of

personal responsibility

in the business community.'

George W. Bush address to the US business leadership
community, July 2002

It must be bad when the President of 'Big Industry Interests'
has to become critical. Someone must have suggested (using
simple language) that falling investor confidence caused by the
dirty deeds of his corporate mates will not be good for Bush
Family plc re-election. It's the ethics of the economy, stupid.

Why else do we need change activist thinking? Our species
and our planet need change activism. Why? Because equality
in the world will remain a dream unless we evolve business
to define its purpose as wider than profit. OK, that sounded
big but it is really simple.

The gulf between business actions and human suffering has
never been greater. We debate 3G technology when half the
population of the world has never made a phone call. Access
to clean water doesn't happen for one in five people on this
planet, and you and I get a new 1-litre sports bottle of Evian.
But don't get me wrong – I am not knocking the benefits. I am
delighted to have my home, my car, my comfortable life and
(after ten years on the breadline) I learned that it is daft to feel
the need to suffer in order to help those who suffer.

Comfort feels good – that's one big reason why capitalism
works. Taking action to extend that comfort to other people feels
even better. Change activism is where you and I come in, to help

evolve capitalism with more balance, more compassion. Change activism is a philosophy of socially inclusive business based on individual actions. Actions, not discussions. It is based on you and I wanting both profit and principles. Forming a formidable community of 'ordinary people', quietly insisting on fairer ways to live and work. We are more in control than we think.

Business co-ordinates the actions of you and I to solve problems every day. In the name of business we create technology networks around the planet, relocate lakes, take oil from the deepest sea beds, etc. That is why I ask you to consider your role. How can you help create an unbeatable combination of business expertise and activist heart, to solve human problems. Take one example, poverty. Every night 800 million people go to bed hungry (*source*: Actionaid); 1.2 billion people live on less than 70p a day. Yet poverty-based hunger is solvable here and now. That's right. We just need to distribute surplus knowledge and food more effectively. We have how many global logistics firms? We have how much food thrown away each day in the West? A quarter of all food purchased in the USA, apparently.

We can choose to broaden the remit of global trade to eliminate hunger. For ever. That is a choice for our generation. Very specifically, a choice for you and I. Imagine each business leader wanting to lead a socially responsible company. Imagine each senior manager working hard to achieve her social objectives, not least because they form part of her performance related pay. If you and I insist (with others just like us), maybe the following story will become normal.

You live on a big estuary. Oil spills into the local river, where your family have fished for generations. The oil refinery five miles away is immediately shut down and a massive clean-up operation takes place. Poisoned oysters and crabs are removed, the oil company re-stocks and pays for the clean-up in a spirit of genuine concern for the well-being of each riverside family. 'Our customers demand environmental justice as an essential part of our global strategy,' commented a spokesman for the oil multinational. One month on, you and your children can eat shellfish, because business was a little less selfish. (If Esso, BP, Shell or any other fossil fuel firm would like to comment on progress, I'd be delighted to write your response in big letters on my website.)

If there's enough shareholder value to be earned from the good deed trade, it's going to happen. If enough employees care enough about reputation and justice, companies will change, if only to stop talent from walking. If enough investors desire a share portfolio of ethically profitable firms, the markets will adapt. If enough customers ask for decently produced trainers – well that campaign worked OK didn't it? Nike and Adidas and Gap and Reebok had to listen when young Americans started to say 'We made you big brand we can break you.' Change activists are powerful.

I wonder if there might be a human analogy to this business case for leaving nature alone? Might we individuals become more productive, successful, happy even if we didn't try to straitjacket our lives into the best economic option? Have you intensively farmed your skills, talent, ideas to the point of reduced harvests? Just a thought.

Change activism is a peaceful revolution. Because of recent protests, you may think activism is the same as rioting. It isn't.

'We've been cooking the books for a long time by leaving out the worth of nature.'

Natural capital (forests, natural ecosystems, e.g. forests, marshes) often returns more left alone, than converted to human use. Based on over 300 case studies, the value of the natural ecosystem – as storm and flood protection, for sustainable hunting and tourism, or to soak up carbon dioxide – outweighed the returns from human use. 'The economics are absolutely stark. We thought the numbers would favour conservatism, but not by that much.' Andrew Balmford, University of Cambridge.

US journal *Science*, 9 August 2002

History shows that peaceful direct action has played a crucial role in bringing about change. Gandhi was an activist. Anita Roddick identifies as an activist.

Change activist definition

A person who takes action outside his or her comfort zone.

Change activist benefits

The ability to create personal profit, with principles.

Finally, change activism makes it happen. The only way to do it is to do it. This book gives you tried and trusted techniques based on both activist and corporate experience, to help you understand activism in its most applicable context – right here and now in your life. There is a case for personal activism to counteract the workplace powerlessness many of us feel.

We need change activism because of where we are. If you don't mind me asking, where are you right now? Do you feel valued at work? Fairly secure about your pensions and investments? Sure you are not onboard some 'dastardly son of Enron'?

Generally, would you say you live a life true to your values? Does your job allow you to create more career options in your life, or less? Do you know your current market value?

Most of us don't have good answers on these big questions – which is OK. But we do need to develop a questioning mind. Change activists ask lots of questions, some more awkward than others, and this book will help you to locate the right questions to get some jucier answers. Isn't it better to know the sometimes painful truth about your life rather than sit still scared and hopeful?

Change activism rings an alarm. I hope loudly, because dreams (yours in particular) could go unrealized unless you shake off the paralysing dust of self-doubt and start believing in your own ability to make big things happen.

We are not schooled in activism, there are just a few people who seem to know their path in life from an early age. Most of us just go with what happens, study whatever we feel we might be good at, get a job somewhere that allows some liveable compromise between paying bills and being creative. We don't ask for too much because who knows, we might get found out as being not especially sure of ourselves.

This passive mindset has collectively led to a few problems. Our jobs don't make us richer unless we happen to co-own the firm. People who work hard for many years see their pensions dwindle. Fair? People who work hard for many years suddenly find out their leaders have played big silly number games with their auditors and this means, sorry, we are going to have to make another 200 redundancies over the next 12 months. Fair? Clearly not. At an individual level, we are

In rows of homes, in well-lit, humming offices, you and I have sat quietly for a long time, hoping it will all work out. It might, but consider the odds. In the first decade of the 21st century, career passivity is a very high-risk approach.

somewhere that means we get up early, stay late, pay bills, pay more bills. And it seems hard to see a way out, other than work harder, win the lottery or take personal control of our lives. Business needs activists. We need to awaken our own personal sense of activism. And as a planet full of little scared animals we need a broader perspective on our activities. Before we leave something nasty for our kids to clean up after us.

What's that got to do with me?

You and I are responsible for how we consume and produce and that means trade is the vehicle for more than global brand management. Business finds form as a mirror of the intent of our senior trade leaders and most powerful consumers. And, ladies and gentlemen on the global economic stage, we are seeing the curtain go up on a major script rewrite. The story of profit motive evolution. From profit by fear and market bullyboy tactics to profit by inclusion. Buy this because it's good for you and me and mother earth. Check it out. It costs more because there are no pesticides. We added 10 per cent because we didn't bankrupt the suppliers. Happy to pay? We increasingly are.

And business has got to be the most adaptable organic organism on the planet. Evolve and survive.

Yes it's a big step. I call it 'trickle down enlightenment'.

As we learn more we can do more. In these early years of the information society, all this new corporate transparency and Web data gives us better, more independent thinking. If we can be bothered. The practical techniques behind change activism are useful for those embarking on a life led by the one living it. In which lovely things happen. This book is for those of you interested in success, profit and principles. It is possible. Now more than ever.

This is a guidebook on the journey to thine own self be true.

It will offer you, your team and your organization tools for change. Activism can bring bigger, better and more impressively moral business results. It is aimed mostly at helping you make career success happen in a way that to thine own self be true. Yes, I know the grammar doesn't work. This is marketing! Thine own self be true. To thine own self be true.

The workplace is a daily playground of moral choices. Some will create a more honest, ethical environment, some will maintain a (not necessarily healthy) status quo. This not too stringent exercise aims to stimulate your thoughts on how you make choices.

Exercise

The change activist spectrum

Consider which answer best describes your own reaction to the following situations.

1. Your boss describes a fun packed corporate entertainment evening he just had with a firm of dodgy (i.e. dishonest) suppliers. Do you:
   a) ask why he chooses that company for a night out and tell him your concerns
   b) ignore it, not anything to do with you, he might turn nasty
   c) tell him he is guilty by association, and you are appalled at his low morals
   d) look into the allegations and consider how best to talk to him once you have some information?

2. You manage an individual or team. Is your managerial philosophy best described as:
   a) give people the basics and let them get on with it
   b) prioritize the tasks that get you noticed at board level
   c) establish common purpose and values

d) do whatever you can to support each person, as long as they seem committed to your agenda?

3. On a late afternoon visit to the department, a senior member of your organization mentions that a number of your colleagues seem to be missing. You know they have gone home early with agreed family commitments. Do you:

a) explain the situation, add that flexible hours have worked well, allowing a more diverse team to flourish

b) tell her that the team do flexi-hours and exit quickly

c) look way into the far horizon beyond her haircut and smile enigmatically

d) tell her it's the *Marie Celeste* after 5.30 and that it's always you that has to turn off the printers as you leave?

Question 1 a) score 3, b) score 1, c) score 2, d) score 4
Question 2 a) score 2, b) score 1, c) score 4, d) score 3
Question 3 a) score 4, b) score 3, c) score 2, d) score 1

My score: Q1_____ Q2_____ Q3_____ Total =

Results

Score 10–15 you try to work from your values, perhaps a change activist in action.

Score 5–10 you are keen to play by whatever works, morally – a change activist within the norms of where you work.

▶

Score 1–5 you are keen to source a number of high
volume shredders – not a change activist by any stretch of
your self-serving imagination.

This isn't scientific!

To your mind and soul

Every job is a compromise and we all trade a bit of happiness
for a bit of economic security. Many of us plan to do what we
most care about outside work. Why is that?

What if there was a way to be more economically effective at
what you most care about? I have a case to make for becoming
active about this assumed trade-off. I believe that we are
ready to earn money at the same time as being happy. Ready
to do well in our jobs at the same time as standing up for
ourselves and things we believe to be important. Who knows,
we may be able to create a better world as well as achieve
personal financial success.

'To me the desire to create and to have control over your
own life, irrespective of the politics of the time or the social
structures was very much part of the human spirit. What I
did not fully realise was that work could open the doors to
my heart.'

Anita Roddick, *Body and Soul*

Your workplace might well be the place to make your dreams come true. However, it's one thing to realize that change is everywhere, consumers are more powerful and that your boss needs you, as much if not more, than you need her. Quite another to change your life. Our modern workplace is still in the historical shadow of the 1950s command and control model. We would heed the voice of our masters in return for job security. 'I will tell you what to do and how much money you can have and in return you make money for me.' For the charity and not-for-profit sectors another model exists – but fundamentally they remain a hierarchy with more of everything at the top, and a bad back from stress further down.

On the other hand witness the movement of social entrepreneurs, people from all walks of life providing human solutions to today's problems. These people work in the not-for-profit sector, in charities, in education and welfare. They speak of the huge changes they could make if only they had access to capital and some free market skills to make the good things happen. And a new hybrid has arrived. Social enterprise, venture philanthropy.

Like some old-fashioned marriage maker I often look at both parties and think how great it would be if they could somehow get together. What might happen if we worked as a true coalition with common purpose? (Common Purpose – a UK charity that does just that is profiled on page 243). The Magic Outcomes programme is one such marriage.[1] Imagine continuing your professional development at the same time as gaining social leadership skills. And delivering tangible

---

See magicsandwich.co.uk

benefit (food, technology, literacy training, better lighting) to people who could really use some of your expertise. My hope is that a new social enterprise concept – let's call it Cause Related Development – could bridge the gap between communities. The Magic Outcomes programme is a social leadership process which enables business people to work for one day a month in a primary school environment, within a structured, mentored development plan. All profits are returned to the school to provide nutrition to the school-children who need fuel for learning. And it gives the individual from business or public sector organization social leadership skills in a way that, frankly, building a raft with the team on some Welsh river cannot ever do.

'To become involved is to reduce your fear.'

Dr Susan Jeffers, *Feel the Fear and Do It Anyway*

Benefits of change activism

Being fluent in project land. Hearing your own music when all around is humming the company tune. Being able to consider all aspects of the day job without flinching at soul level.

There's a pretty big challenge for those who want to be the best brand in the marketplace. Which follows directly from being the best individual brand in the sales department, the production department (or whatever your departments are called).

Change activism creates a mindset that actively seeks the transition, and can therefore lead in a marketplace where the second to market offering frequently isn't going to survive. In the chaos of new products or services you need to be making things happen, fast. Rather than writing a report on what the competition just did.

I sometimes felt in company life that management was like leadership, only less effective. Change activism is fast change: from the heart change.

What happens when we take top tactics from social activism – the things that got Greenpeace on to prime-time news – into the workplace? What might happen? Taking this one stage further – what if we gave ourselves the time we give our employers – in our heads? The thoughts you choose to think today at your desk might be the springboard for everything you've ever wanted to achieve in your career. Do you under-estimate how much more you could do for yourself?

'What are the business benefits of an activist mindset? Unbelievable! You feel better, you look better, you make more money, you have more friends (clients), you laugh more, you cry more, you grow faster, you strive harder, you see more, believe more, you are bigger, better . . . different! And people – clients, employees, associates and suppliers – all want to be part of the magic you are making!'

Sue Maguire, Founder, Ideas Unlimited

Instead of being passive – at worst playthings for our employers to direct – this book will show you how to use an array of tried and trusted methods to get yourself pointed towards the goals you want to achieve. Without compromising. Staying true to the things that matter to you. If you're interested in getting more of what you want from your life – come with me.

And you should listen to me because?

I hope to help you learn about change activism because it works, it integrates the head, heart and hand and it will help you get what you want. It won't always be easy but you will be alert and awake during the years you're alive. Is that OK with you sir?

I have been alive for 41 years and so far spent eight years as a full-time social activist. Campaigning. Being an anti-nuclear activist. Getting involved in anti-racism work. Standing up for the things I believe are morally right.

I made the odd migration from activist to corporate. I became a secretary, and then an IT project manager (it was a good employer) and found that the activist tools I had learned along the way translated well. Focus, passion, integrity and stamina – that sort of stuff – helped projects go in early, below budget. I got good reviews. I got promoted fast; the company paid for my MBA. Another company hired me for much more money and about then I realized anywhere focused solely on short-term profit figures was never going to be a true home. So I started my own business – and stumbled a bit, learned how to reach and keep great clients, had more success from the same inclusive principles.

For the past ten years life has been inside corporations: an IT manager, a change management consultant, running programmes for big companies. Seeing what works and what doesn't work. Watching the same old reactions when the boss says, 'We need to change. Let's run a programme.' Mass groans. 'Who wants to be on this very crucial, critical, vital, exciting programme?' Hide from boss time. Pretend to have very urgent phone conversations when he walks past . . .

More recently I've spent time as a business coach, helping people discover what is most important to them and to get their life pointed at their priorities. I found a growing tribe of socially minded bankers, caring new technologists, environmentalist fund managers, ethical scientists, who all had a common quest. A life of greater work and life balance. A life with some social contribution as well as professional and material success. . I want to help more people feel more successful and more able to contribute to the world around them. Beyond the bottom line.

My experience has been that as an activist – at heart – I got business success.

The things I learned from that time and from the non-violent campaigns I worked on in later years gave me fantastic education in activist management.

My personal checklist for making things happen:

- Know who you are and what matters to you.
- Get clear on what you want to happen.
- Picture success in your mind's eye.

- Be passionate!

- Ask: is it important and worthwhile?

- Work out allies and get a coalition together.

- Don't forget your loved ones and a good night out!

- Give the media a good story.

- Ask for help from experienced and important people.

- Be very persistent when people say maybe.

- Expect to go off course on a regular basis before you get there!

How can you get the same benefits in your life? Decide to think differently about your day-to-day routines. Expect **But is it possible? Yes. How?** to go outside your comfort zone. Support yourself using techniques from the activist toolkit. Dare to be in control of your thoughts and therefore your life – because taking control is the heart and soul of activism and is what makes the activist so powerful.

Passion + principles + purpose = sustainable success

Activists taking control involves some pretty effective techniques – it isn't easy to persuade a multinational about anything other than making money. It isn't easy, to use a recent example, to highlight the perils of genetically modified food – without some passion and principles and purpose. Being vigilant for profit-versus-people activity does annoy those who stand to gain. Which is what makes it so important for some people to discredit everything to do with activism.

Why would I want to talk to the business community? Am I a traitor to the cause? I wondered about that – and the conclusion I came to is that as I'm passionate about building a crusade within trade against poverty and injustice, it seems sensible to publicize the links between change activism and successful business. Which I repeatedly want to set in a moral and ethical context. Because there is so much more happening than the next e-mail, or what your boss might be moving onto after this project. There is more.

A whole world more.

And potentially – if you're interested – there is a jackpot of money and ethics waiting to be claimed by those of us who can get above the noise of surviving corporate life. The tools I learned gave me the kind of headstart on success that I would dearly love others to have.

So this is passing on stuff that works, as well as some encouragement. It's not easy to find the courage to be moral, assertive and still make it in a material world.

Your contribution level = your fulfilment level

Here is a quick look at what has led me to this moment.

1982. I'm with a group of women weaving a web of wool, outside on the grassy verge at the entrance to USAF Greenham Common. We select photographs of our families and loved ones to indicate why we're taking action to protest against the nuclear missiles, lying in their concrete silos behind us in the base. We show images from all over the world. Our diverse coalition, learning from each other about the interconnectedness of all things. And strangely we have some fun as well. Learning to support each other as we took risks for the issues we believed in. Expecting to win, not even thinking we couldn't. Trusting that we could handle whatever happened.

1990. In a meeting room at the offices of British Telecom, discussing holistic management, proposing that the human body and the corporate body are parallel and that mind that body and spirit equate to strategy, operations and culture. And they all integrate for best performance. Very excited about this.

1995. Five years later, have proved the holistic management concept in practice, now a conference speaker, describing how to integrate improvements using revolutionary method called trust.

2000. Setting up a series of Web-based seminars to show how change in the business world depends on our ability to transcend a mindset of hierarchy and struggle. Helping firms trade with trust, adding value beyond the bottom line and seeing profit from morality. Teaching about diversity as a source of competitive advantage. Starting the Magic Sandwich project; to redistribute perhaps one hundredth of the e-business budget of a few investment banks into a school breakfast scheme, starting in London.

2002. Working on the Magic Sandwich child poverty project. We've just completed the first year, delivering food to five East London primary schools. Working with a great team on a social leadership programme called 'Magic Outcomes'. Our goal is to show how a social enterprise working with big business can solve child hunger – our profit goes to primary schools, to buy nutritious food for the children, as fuel for learning. (More on this in Chapter Three or see magicsandwich.co.uk.)

From the web to the Web. A diverse coalition to managing diversity. Almost a circle. And the constant themes have been keep learning, try out stuff, trust more, worry less.

From Greenham to Greenspan

As a lifelong change activist I am realistic about what can be achieved by heartfelt appeals to the business community sense of moral rightness. Some people can see that polluting the oceans is a bad idea. Some can't. Same with child slavery. Same with racist e-mails on your Intranet. We sustain a mixture of priorities in the business community. Heroes and villains and most of us trying to do our best in the middle.

I did my time standing outside unethical business with a placard saying please stop. Eventually I decided it would be much better to be inside at the table, where I could make some audible intervention. And being honest, there came a point in my life when I wanted somewhere warm and easier and salaried.

Enlightened – meaning fair and sustainable – global capitalism is probably our best chance of reducing poverty, promoting economic growth and increasing the well-being of our fellow humans around the world. Despite the nagging sense that fair capitalism might be a big fat oxymoron.

There is an unravelling of unaccountable power taking place before our eyes. For sure. A new generation of business leaders will create better integrated and human business systems – because that is the next stage of capitalist evolution. As that happens perhaps the stage will be set for individuals in their employ to also shape their lives. Could this be a major turning point in our global economy?

The reason for my undying optimism is this. Trade does what we (the consumer, aka 'the markets') tell it to. No one but us running the world, so the good news is we can do something about it. The good news is, we can make changes by using our collective and individual voices. Thank goodness it isn't down to accounting magic (Circa 2002, dead and gonsky) or the gods of the sea or Alan Greenspan, chief of the US Federal Reserve Board. You thought it was? OK then, here comes the individual level cause and effect shift. It's down to the person reading these words. Right now.

chapter two

change activism can strengthen your bottom line

why does your firm need change activism, now?

THE DAYS of the boss having all the answers are over. Trust is going to replace fear because trust is more effective and cheaper. Market pace needs speed of light decisions, taken by people who are then courageous enough to act. Even if that means changing the way things have been done before.

The day-to-day journey of career progress integrates with our homelife, our society and our personal development path.

Companies that encourage people who match the change activist profile are more likely to react at the speed necessary to compete.

We see our careers move and get redesigned and restructured. Endlessly. Part of an organic moving whole, it seems, without a permanent anchor.

Fluency with change is a skill that enables us to make choices with less fear, to cope with new situations and to be thrilled at the chance to try some new stuff. Chance fluency should be taught alongside reading, writing and artithmetic. It's essential.

And within business, there's still a sense that decisions that cause change can be made only at the top of the organization. But waiting for the word of the gods on your board, high up on the status tree, risks leaving your business dead in the ground. There is a significant business downside in leading only from the top.

I grew up (corporately) in a time of matrix management, in project organizations where we expected to handle a fair amount of market-based change in addition to business as usual. Empowered 'programme managers' kept the flotilla of ambitious and hungry project managers – the change agents – focused and directed. The programme managers – usually more experienced and higher up the status tree. They reported to the board. The board had a traditional structure with most decisions left to the hero leader CEO managing director. Ultimately.

Many projects that had connection to the customer need simply withered on the vine due to delays in getting decisions from the status tree. The project manager spotted something – a real gap in the market to be exploited. OK, do it, said the programme manager – if it costs less than £100,000. More than that I gotta take it to the board. The project manager, feeling less than trusted and empowered, waited for the big board-level decision.

The board – aka the least well-qualified people in the building when it comes to market need right here right now. Years of climbing and strategizing left them with a woefully underdeveloped sense of the average consumer and they relied on teams of advisers. Some of whom were brave but only to the point of career survival. None dared jeopardize the car/mortgage/credit card payments. Who of us would?

So what happens? The project manager took action slowly. Perhaps in some markets it would have been fine. Manufacturing ketchup perhaps. But – given the speed of the technology market – chances are, some faster competitor sniffed out the same niche and grabbed it.

Birds evolved successfully from dinosaurs, becoming one of the most prevalent species on the planet. Fish have managed to diversify beyond our calculation. They don't rely on one pair of sensory alert systems to watch for danger, keep predators at bay. They either have a system of watchers or everyone watches equally.

So what am I advocating? That we create a strange activist culture with employees doing their own thing regardless of strategy or budget? That the board takes trust and learning speed as seriously as budgets and status?

Yep, I am. But it must be consistent activism. Consistent with the activism of the marketplace.

Developing a firm of change activists will paradoxically probably mean a lot of talking at first. And it isn't easy to win hearts: just ask the big firms desperate for their IT contractors to join. I advocate winning hearts, building coalitions and working with your employees based on what is mutually valuable. Which I agree takes time.

But look at the options. Change by fear? The floggings will continue until morale improves. Or market advantage by spying. Oracle's CEO Larry Ellison owned up that his firm payed for 'corporate intelligence' to rummage in Bill Gates's rubbish to find evidence helpful to the US government (oh yes – and second place Oracle) in their anti-trust case against Microsoft.

'In corporate America, what's ethical is what's legal,' according to one interview in the *Wall Street Journal*. But not profitable. JP Morgan's technology analyst marked Oracle stock down to 'market performer', i.e. a hold rather than buy stock, following negative feedback from the Oracle spy story.

Most people – if trusted by their company and directed to do something achieveable and useful – will add loads of value.

Market tip: buy trust sell fear

Corporate leaders who can state their objectives clearly and live by values that are authentic and visible tend to grow the kind of employee commitment necessary for fast market response.

By contrast, companies where the boss thinks give them an inch and they'll take the photocopier don't generally drum up world-beating performance. Bully cultures perform even worse. Yes, you get short-term action while people manage for their dear lives. We all scramble when we feel we have no choice. Then first chance, good people get out.

I had a chat the other day with a very experienced programme manager for large construction projects. Multimillion dollar stuff. He was describing how he controls the programme using data. For example, he can see the efficiency of his programmes by reference to a cost/time schedule. If the project has a positive cost variance he's happy. If not it's action time.

He proceeded to tell a recent anecdote. One day his chart showed rising project costs and decreased productivity. I could explain the concept of earned value if you like. You don't like? OK.

The chart showed the project moving into financial loss. Which is career limiting on a multi-million construction programme, right? Materials were costing more and the team producing less progress. His reaction? 'So I rang the factory boss up and said – 'what the hell is going on'? I made him sweat, I can tell you.'

I think he thought our little circle would be impressed with his firm management style. But the problems had probably arisen because of his firm management style. And over-reliance on data.

The fear not trust approach had just about run the project into crisis. What do I mean by that? Well, imagine you run the factory, and find out some materials are likely to be late, leading to downtime for lots of expensive resources. Machine doesn't arrive. People are sitting around doing nothing. And you know your programme manager is the kind of guy inclined to a bout of shouting down the phone. What are you going to do? Call him sooner and get him near cardiac incident when the materials might arrive anyway. No way. You wait and hope. And then give it one more day with everything crossed. And then guess what? Next thing it's overdue and you don't know what to say about why you didn't call earlier.

It's called being human. Not wanting horrible things to happen during the working day.

So – the guy sitting in his office gets the data, plots the chart, makes the overheated phone call. Factory manager squirms, apologizes. Gets that familiar acid pain in his stomach.

Meanwhile no machine. People are sitting around. Project budget overruns. Potential time delays. Construction manager not happy.

There was another way. To trust that the factory manager also wanted early delivery on the project. That he or she was trying just as hard as senior mangement to make the project come in to time, cost and performance specifications. This would have led to a more communications-based project control method – instead of relying on a chart with retrospective data. For the construction manager to go around 'catching people doing things right' as one of my ex-managers used to call it. Expecting good things and encouraging open discussion. For example, to have a chat every week where problems could be aired, so improving visibility of potential issues. So if there was a danger of delay on materials – the factory manager would have brought it up. Early. And the programme manager could have escalated it with the machine supplier, or put the resources on another piece of work. And the whole into loss situation could have been averted.

And I wonder how many times the 'too scared to call' thing goes on. Firms where a senior manager makes all the decisions, and is such an ego (remember egos are overheads) that he/she can't trust the team and has to have all the infor-mation as hard data – always retrospectively. And no one can say when a problem might happen because they'll have their face removed and put up as a trophy. Business just can't afford it. And for crying out loud, can't we humans do better in terms of how we spend our days?

Is it about fear or trust?

Some companies are still fuelled by fear. Big bosses with big sticks keep control and check and you don't ever bother with that hippy thing called feedback. Some companies are fuelled by relationships. Some companies are based on trust. So given that we all get a bit close to our lives, here is a handy little checklist to find out.

Quiz

What fuels my workplace?

Is it a) fear b) relationships c) trust?

Mark 2 points for every yes, 1 point for every maybe or sometimes, and 0 for a clear no. Then add up your scores and see below.

Workplaces run on fear

How can you tell if your workplace runs on fear?	Circle which is most true for you	If you said yes, this is what might be happening
You feel lucky to work for such a good firm – of course you don't mind that there's no bonus	Yes I do No I don't	Equity for owners/ shareholders only
There's lots of emphasis on production targets and reports	Yes that's right No not really	Data management – potentially low emotional intelligence
You only talk to people in the same department	Yes I do I talk to everyone	Functional – narrow focus
Your business card has your rank, title and postcode on it	Yes it does Not it doesn't	Status is all

How can you tell if your workplace runs on fear?	Circle which is most true for you	If you said yes, this is what might be happening
It can be scary to talk to the boss – and you always need an appointment	That's right Not true	Command and control
You work hard, play hard. And hope the pension will come soon	Yes I do. You bet! How sad. Not true	Macho management. A lot of people suffocate in the testosterone tunnel
You don't have time for training	That's right Not true	You de-skill and lose options to move on or up
You find your senior managers very amusing and wonderful in a party situation	They can be very witty Not true. Ever ...	The company line rules
Boss is proud not to use a PC	True enough Nope	Technology averse, meaning your communication is limited by timezones and location
There aren't many people around who are not clones of the senior team	Yep We have a very diverse team around here	Diversity averse. Very unhelpful when serving global markets
It takes guts to put new ideas forward	Definitely Not at all	Innovation suffers

So remember to score each one and add up your score.

yes = 2 points

maybe = 1 point

no = 0 points

Score 16–22 Are you sure you want to stay in your current workplace? Chances are you're not getting the development you need, you may well feel underconfident, you certainly don't get the chance to voice your own ideas as you should. You are somewhere that may not evolve fast enough to survive. Your workplace is likely to be bad for your career and activists say go!

Score 6–15 There's is an element of freedom that perhaps makes your place remain bearable – perhaps you get paid well, or there's a sexy brand on the wall. What are the risks of asking for more openness, more diversity? If the job is evolving, fine. If this is as good as it gets maybe you deserve better.

Score 0–5 Congrats. You don't work somewhere fuelled by fear. So what's stopping you really making a big impact? Go for it!

'Humankind has not woven the web of life. We are but one thread within it. Whatever we do to the web, we do to ourselves. All things are bound together. All things connect.'

Chief Seattle

People want to work in an inspiring environment where something greater than cash gets generated. Not all – but a lot of us. *Built to Last* – the best-selling book by James Collins and Gerry Porras (Random House, 1998) – shows how longstanding companies with core values and a desire for more than just profit do beat those companies that have nothing more than profit motive. They considered hundreds of companies in the most rigorous academic way and found that timeless concepts such as clarity of purpose, core values and the ability to keep learning create outstanding financial growth and performance. And yes of course I would put that in because it backs my arguments. The book is as near as you'll get to objective proof that values make sustainable profits. There are many companies in there that don't stand up well to our new consumer ethics standard – but no one can deny the evidence that core values and a desire to make more than profit have been major contributors to long-term success.

Shared commitment to change and shared values can develop the kind of trust necessary to fast-track the big business decisions – in essence have them taken on trust. Guanxi (a Chinese word meaning trust and mutual honour) has proved critical in the expansion of business throughout the Asia Pacific region. Trust. Not contracts. Leadership and the ability to take action at all levels of the organization based on trust.

One of the key findings from *Built to Last* is this:

'Just about anyone can be a key protagonist in building an extraordinary business institution. The lessons of these companies can be learned and applied by the vast majority of managers at all levels. Gone forever – at least in our eyes – is the debilitating perspective that the trajectory of a company depends on whether it is led by people ordained with rare and mysterious qualities that cannot be learned by others.'

Collins and Porras

It takes us ordinary people, using our extraordinary gifts of passion and purpose, to make things happen. Every ordinary week. Leading the firm through the kind of change essential to survive. Change isn't about getting the board together with some expensive consultants at a nice venue. It's about harnessing the best of our humanity. And one key aspect of future business success is the ability to find and motivate the activists.

Business needs the brainpower of passionate, powerful, practical people. So – back to you. Your firm needs you to be a change activist. What can you do – what help exists to get there? In some ways leadership and change activism are the self-same things. Many companies don't really want either. But I can show that the world-beaters have an innate method for creating both.

What change programme?

Is it reasonable to assume that part of your job is to help your company manage change? If that is the case your duties will range from project management to spying. Apparently.

Have you been on any good briefings, project start-ups or team meetings recently? Did you talk about the need for change? To in-source previously outsourced divisions? Six sigma workshop perhaps? Joint ventures for beginners? How did you feel? Yes we can do it? Or nasty sinking feeling of been there done that? Oh, you had that same old sinking feeling? You are not alone.

"Never choose a mission statement on a dark, rainy day?"

We are still midway through the 'let's start a project' wave of change window dressing. Yes, I said window dressing. Most change efforts based around the project lifecycle don't aim for lasting, profound change. They aim for fix it now while we have a budget and a sponsor in one place for a while. So how does anybody move beyond the tide of business as usual to make something new happen? Oh. We have only one offering still. Projects, right? Specially designed by heroic change athletes to give more urgency to your work than business as usual. The staple fix-it tool for pretty much all company problems for a while.

But what are they again? In my best corporate voice I can say that projects are defined as a unique series of actions, with clear time cost and performance specifications. With a team that in most organizations gets organized as a matrix to cause maximum accountability for the project manager and the team, with minimum responsibility. Comment? It is true.

A posse of projects equals one change programme. A clutch of change programmes from nowhere may mean your firm has just been taken over.

There's a huge amount of hyperbole about embracing change, loving the whitewater, urging the future forward and marketing it into some consumer's face. And some people are making lots of money from it.

Change management consultancy, for example, has been a huge boom area. Management consulting fees have grown year on year for years. Why? Because hard-pressed, deeply stressed executives seem to need the comfort blanket of a bright consultant saying there's a methodology for handling change. And because the money you spend as a client doesn't come from your own pocket. As someone who has worked in exactly this area I've noted a less than delirious welcome for the consultants promising cultural clarity and senior team cohesion. Client: 'Where did you achieve that before – exactly?' 'Oh – the programme achieved it's goals partially . . .' The experience of change consultants can – indeed has been – a valuable support to senior teams seeking large-scale improvements. But let's be real. Very few firms have really achieved original change programme expectations with or without external help. The biggest change programme is one that will convince business leaders that mergers and acquisitions don't work, to tell the users that large IT implementations will be over time, over budget with less functionality. The change activist difference is to plan and implement customer-led, employee pleasing business change over a period of time. To build trust, not just cut employee numbers and self-esteem in half, take the bonus and go – that strategy spectacularly failed at AOL-Time Warner, WorldCom and

Anyone Believing Mr B. Ebbers. Maybe a better plan is in place at HP-Compaq. How's that one going?

Kotter – why change fails

According to John Kotter, Matsushita Professor at Harvard, based on top 100 company research, there are eight main reasons why companies fail at big change initiatives:

1. Failing to establish sense of urgency – crises and opportunities.

2. Not forming a powerful guiding coalition – enlisting adequate senior sponsorship.

3. Not creating a vision – developing strategies to get there.

4. Not communicating the vision – teaching new behaviours.

5. Failing to empower others – getting others to act.

6. Not planning for and getting short-term wins – visible improvements.

7. Failing to consolidate improvements.

8. Not managing to instititutionalize improvements.

Looking at this list, many key factors boil down to an inability at the top to get passionate enough, create a common purpose and coalition. For many senior teams change is going to happen out there. When it first needs to happen in here. Inside the person leading the organization.

I was delighted to read that the CEO of Coca-Cola (Mr D. Daft when I last looked) said he wanted activists to drink Coke on their protests, rather than throw Coke bottles. Now I don't, repeat, don't, agree with violent protest. And Coke is fine as fizzy drinks go. But given Daft's desire to have activists as a targettable niche, here is a speech by Nelson Mandela in May 2000, which, if Daft chooses to respond, could really appeal to us.

'Surely when children and adolescents in every part of the world can name their favourite soft drink, running sports shoe, we are able to ensure that they will have access to the information they need to stay healthy. In a world that so often decries the apathy of its youth we can open our arms for the millions of adolescents eager to contribute their new ideas and bounding enthusiasm . . .

'But now amid growing economic interdependence among nations we see a new global reality with additional protago-nists including non-governmental organizations, grassroots groups, private enterprise, the business community and other diverse groups.'

Nelson Mandela, On Building a Global Partnership For Children,
Johannesburg, 6 May 2000

Did I hear him say Coca-Cola come on down if you really want to help in the world? How much do you make? How much can you share? I'm sure a little bit more. I was interested to read that Coca-Cola *do* support initiatives in Africa. But it stops a long way short of each sub-Saharan Cola van carrying water and essential vaccines as well as sugar and fizz. So how about it? Show me you give a substantial percentage of profit and I'd like to teach the world to drink Coke along with the best of them. In my humble view, Coke PR/greenwash is as soul affirming as Coke is teeth affirming. Contact me if I can help, Mr Daft.

How activist thinking brings business benefits

The headlines

- Simply doing the job more effectively, juicing performance with values.

- Helping the company find its higher self and more money by ethical branding.

- Building revenue streams for yourself based on what you really want to do.

Simply doing the job more effectively

So we tentatively take control and responsibility for our lives. We acknowledge the impact of our thinking on our actions. We know what's important to us and want to live our lives based on our values. We make things happen. We're getting to be change activists.

'This is a bad time for people who don't like change.'

Johan Stael von Holstein, CEO, Letsbuyit.com *Sunday Times*
Net Heads column, 23 April 2000

Helping the company find its higher self and more money by ethical branding

There would appear to be a virtuous circle in place. The best-led firms get the best people and attract greater investment and develop great products, which the public loves, which brings revenue, which enables them to do bigger things and so on. There is certainly greater recognition that the firm or public organization has an intangibly valued 'good name' to defend. Brands are weakened or strengthened by a number of factors – including perception of how the organization manages ethical, environmental and social issues. There is a growing realization that managing the organization needs to include an element of social responsibility. The London Stock Exchange combined code on corporate governance now states that directors should deal with non-financial risks, such as health and safety, the environment and risk to reputation. The phrase 'triple bottom line' is gaining ground (coined by John Erhlington MD, Sustainability). This refers to measurement of social and environmental progress as well as financial rewards. A growing number of firms, including British Telecom, the Co-Operative Bank and The Body Shop declare their annual reports in terms of the triple bottom line. Something to consider at individual and team level as well, perhaps.

But for most private firms results are relatively short term, and financial. The vein of contribution that *Built to Last* showed to be so powerful has yet to become mainstream. Although there is a whole pageful of books on Amazon called *Beyond the Bottom Line*, perhaps reflecting the reasonable expectation that human beings should be treated with respect in business. These days it's hard to find a public spokesperson for treating people poorly in the workplace. Spin management rather than funda-mental change perhaps. But on a good day I feel that we might be entering a time of social evolution when it will be possible to trust that the ethical will be recognized as the surest and most enjoyable path to the profitable.

'The benefits of having a activist mentality are:

Knowledge: encourages one to network and build up a support base in a company

Knowledge: encourages one to engage others in ideas and across boundaries

Creativity: helps develop creative approaches to challenges

Persistence: helps get things done despite barriers, helps recognise that one failure is not a failure of the Idea, but only of that attempt and that from that one can learn and make the next attempt more effective

Proactive: act in stealth mode from the formal power holder until it is necessary to make it public

Planning: always thinking in terms of contingencies and what could go right and wrong

Integrity: don't compromise principles/purpose in pursuit of objective

Money: helps get things done well on a lean budget

Employee satisfaction: helps engage people's participation based on non-monetary rewards but with "people rousing" skills.'

Duane Raymond, Founder of Fairsay.com

Mark Blanchard, a manager working in Zurich Financial Services, wrote to say how he had applied change activist concepts with success, in his workplace.

'Although "Activists" are individuals those same attributes can be applied to any business. I looked at (Retail Financial Services) RFS Claims and in the course of a re-structure considered whether the energy levels were generally high or low, whether the culture was based on trust and the extent of our combined emotional intelligence. Healthy individuals and a healthy work-place make for better performance.

The re-structure looked at integration of two types of business and it was important to understand not only the physical connects but the cultural connects, which are often over-looked. Human value was put high on the agenda. Simple steps were taken to ensure that any discomfort was managed in a positive way. We made sure that:

The objectives were clear and understood.

We developed key performance indicators for every member of staff so that they could identify the objective with their real work.

We engaged the entire management team in the change programme and as many staff as possible within the decision making process.

We created the role of the change activist to overcome any immediate barriers and helped to influence others to breakdown those barriers. We started a programme of twinning to ensure people across all sites were talking (no silo mentality, thank you).

The energizer comes next to help sustain those energy levels. The key to its success was to recognise that people matter and it is the people that make it happen.'

Mark Blanchard, Technical Claims Manager, Retail Financial Services,

Zurich Financial Services

Kyosei and Canon

Canon, the Japanese cameras to photocopiers multinational, has over 67,000 employees. It's the world's largest producer of photocopiers. Its laser printers have over 70 per cent of global market share. The underlying philosophy is kyosei, literally meaning symbiosis. It's the word chosen by the late Ryuzaburo Kaku president of Canon from 1989 to 1999, to describe the sense of global corporate responsibility. He interprets kyosei as 'living and working together for the common good of mankind'. Kaku believes that business needs a global philosophy for the twenty-first century, and believes his company is putting it into action.

Kaku felt the new century would have only four types of business:

- those that are purely capitalistic, interested only in profit, and caring little for employee welfare

- those that have good labour relations and share profits with workers

- those that look to the interests of all 'stakeholders' including employees, shareholders, customers, suppliers and the wider community

- those that have a sense of global responsibility.

The last type, he said, aims to tackle 'global imbalances' in trade relations and job opportunities, in the gap between rich and poor nations, and in the quality of the environment that today's generation leaves for the next. The US journal, *Business Ethics*, wrote that: 'Kaku's kyosei is gaining an international following. One reason is that it seems to work, both in terms of improving social and environmental conditions and in making a more profitable business.'

The new president at Canon is equally committed to kyosei and, given the enormous economic clout Canon has at its disposal, their call for business responsibility is all the more significant. (Thanks to Michael Smith, quotes first published in *Beyond the Bottomline*, 2000, The Industrial Pioneer.)

Let's do diversity

There are firms that right now are waking up to the fact that not everyone who wants a job is exactly the same. That being true to oneself is sometimes hard in a workplace where it's easier to be just like the others. The management buzzterm is valuing diversity. This has come about for two reasons. First because there is no longer the secure supply channel feeding the corporate need for screen fodder. Resources equals

© 1999 Randy Glasbergen. www.glasbergen.com

"Our office has been dominated to receive an award for Diversity In The Workplace!"

business transactions equals profit. So some of us human resources, breathing assets, whatever you want to call a person who needs to go to work are now becoming a tiny bit prized in some circles.

Investment banking is one of them. There is a huge drive to recruit and retain resources in the many complex technology-driven jobs within the financial services industry. And banks are having a hard time filling them. You think I'm joking, right? Investment banks, big bucks for long hours and no problem with a nice identity pitch? Wrrrrong. Five years ago no problem. Today problem. Not everyone wants long hours and being on call all weekend and all that for income and status. I know – it seems odd to me too – but that's probably a generation thing.

So reason one for valuing diversity is resource shortage. Diversity wasn't an issue while the white boys in suits were freely available. Nope. Nor is there a post-millennium rise in board-level desire for equality of opportunity for all employees. Nope.

Reason two is the bad press caused by lawsuits. Employees being sent racist e-mails. Employees who had to listen to pornographic stories in the open plan office. Those people sued and sued big and the financial payout was the least damaging part. An investment bank – in a time of increasingly integrated global markets – can't afford to say this is a great place to work as long as your skin is white and you're not a woman. There are too many other places to work if you have the skills. So diversity has become a very hot to trot management issue. And that's why so many major corporations suddenly have diversity programmes, funded by HR's newest role – the diversity champion. Where the competition for skills is most apparent, and there's a measurable correlation between screen fodder (oh sorry, members of our IT team) and trading volumes, you get a fertile breeding ground for 'we really value our people.' When you're a senior manager in a major division that doesn't look like it will hit its financial targets because people keep leaving to work some place better – then diversity becomes an issue. Where skills are easy to find and retain, and the job is more operational in nature, guess what. You'll be told to hurry back from the bathroom and no you can't leave early because your child is sick. I know there are exceptions but we're dealing with the early stages of enlightened business and the joys of supply and demand are not under critical mass moral scrutiny.

Diversity is a litmus test. How does your senior team check out?

In some firms diversity is driven from the top and the board are genuine about wanting to build a meritocracy and being truly open and honest about the historical imbalances that exist in every workplace. There are some fantastic initiatives trying to ensure a more fair and open workplace. But it's always driven by the business imperative – being able to recruit and retain the best person. Now with the add on – from a diverse slate.

One investment banker – a senior guy in technology – recently told me that he'd spent ages trying to find a female senior IT expert to present at a recruitment day. 'We just don't have any women at the top in technology.' Wonder why? With only one female chief executive of a UK FTSE 100 (Marjorie Scardino) and just as few in the USA, no wonder so many women leave the institution to its insurmountable history and go it alone. A high percentage of start-ups are female owned. A high percentage of small to medium-size enterprises are run by women. Breathing their own air outside the testostorone tunnels of senior corporate life.

Now I think of it, why were many of the financial accounting scandals whistleblown by women, e.g. Enron and Andersen. Why do you think that happened? Surely being ethical and wonderful, is a human thing. It doesn't come in just one outer coating of gender or colour or shoe size, in my view. But when I look at the 2002 G8 summit delegates, or the Institute of Directors annual meeting or the *Sunday Times* Rich List or the British Medical Council convention – well, call me a radical feminist, but isn't there a disproportionate number of lads in them there photos? Just a bit out of alignment with they society they seek to serve?

I used to have a postcard on my desk (when I was an IT project manager in a telecoms firm) saying 'a woman wanting to be the equal of a man lacks ambition'. I had it framed when my manager told me to put it away. 'You ain't seen nothing yet sweet thing.' I remember him not liking that Post-it message either.

Does your organization treat different people differently? Let's take one example – gay people – welcome where you work or gently encouraged to keep it all quiet? JP Morgan have for some time sponsored the gay and lesbian campaigns group, Stonewall Equality, dinner in London. JP Morgan is a very good, very serious investment banker. Why do they bankroll a queer campaigning organization? There's also a group within JP Morgan called **Respect for diversity is but** GLEAM (Gay and Lesbian **one example of the** Employees at Morgan), origi- **growth of to thine own self** nally founded in the US HQ. I **be true in the workplace.** spoke to members in London – wanting to understand how they were able to brave the potential backlash from 'small c' (i.e. conservative) financial services. The senior team at JP Morgan does seem to have worked out that a workplace where people can be themselves is good for business. Gay men and lesbians welcomed as equal and visible contributors to the culture is a big step forward in the context of financial services conservatism.

I've seen that this openness to diversity being led from the top at JP Morgan is causing some changes in company image and positioning. The company is now seen as leading the diversity debate among investment banks. For example, their recruitment ads don't always carry white male faces any more. And competitors are doing the same. And maybe that means that more people will join – over time creating critical mass of change activists who are treated well – even when true to themselves.

There's a clear and ringing business truth emerging. Firms that encourage people to be themselves, rather than act out some role for the senior audience, are likely to reap the rewards in terms of loyalty and performance.

If you want competitive advantage, try to identify the masks you have to maintain in order to do well in the organization. For example, do you feel you have to: 'be the boss who knows all answers', 'be the new person who has to understand instructions through telepathy rather than risk asking questions' or 'dress like an American college student when you much prefer a chalwa chamiz'? Check it out.

Less layers. Means more happy players. And 'to thine own self be true' is the foundation for good stakeholder management. Let's say you try playing by the old rules of divide, rule and don't let shareholders in the same room as the employees. Only now instead of two stakeholders there are ten. How can you keep morphing into the yes man for lots of diverse stakeholders and still keep your 'you are my biggest priority' story straight? Transparency demands integrity. There aren't enough hours in the day to keep anything but the truth in circulation. And we consumers are getting increasingly keen on truth.

Truthful companies are also more likely to have the kind of structure within which people feel free to create. Take 3i for instance. Internal slush funds for your business plans. If it works – you get a share of the action. If it fails – great you tried out an idea.

In one fairly well-known example, an employee wondered how less than totally adhesive glue might be put to practical use and put forward an idea for reminder notes with moderately powerful adhesive. Not expecting much to come of it apparently. I use Post-it notes every-day and once ran a workshop where a senior team worked out a new distribution strategy using them! How do you encourage in-house entrepreneurialism? How many new business ideas arrive on the MD's desk every week?

Change activists tend to leave big corporates if they feel creatively or morally stifled.

Creative or moral limitation also means a cap on learning and fluency. Which longer term equals capped financial rewards. Established large telecoms firms, for example, have seen an increasing amount of attrition to the new market entrants. After years of a hierarchy with carrot and stick motivation, the big firms are waking up to the benefits of intrinsic motivation. The value of the work itself, of itself. Which does your firm encourage? Corporates recognize the contribution of change activists especially in areas such as business development, doing deals, spotting new product opportunities. And want to keep those who can make change happen very happy. What makes you happy about your job? The change activist in you wants to ask for more of what makes you happy – or perhaps just get on with it.

So if you're a senior manager and wondering what kind of people to recruit, think about it. Do you want people in your organization who care about improving the firm and feel able to live by their own values 'to thine own self be true'? Are you open enough to debate the grey areas? Are you big enough? Because they'll probably take you on with any moral inconsistencies, for the benefit of quality and learning, trust and all that good stuff. And will give a lot because they believe in the worth of the work. It also costs more not to look after people in your organization. Simple things like recruitment and training costs when people leave, unhappy, after a year or two. Simple things like the loss of good will and consistency. Firms with a strong product, up-front moral code and a recognition of 'thine own self be true and not just at the upper levels of the company' do well.

Personal to corporate. Don't even risk being unethical

Being ethical gains consumer brownie points.

We hear that youth culture desires greater expression of individuality. Groups like Adbusters and the rising numbers of ethical fund managers question the conformism of brands and demand corporate accountability. The trade is that firms branding on authenticity get better youth consumer support. This is undoubtedly influenced by the likes of Nike being hit by US campus protests. But what is the link between ethics and profitability? Simply that in a faster market trustworthiness becomes a shorthand for good management practice, which is a good indicator of performance. The company that bothers to put the processes and senior focus in place to do a triple bottom line (environment, social and financial) report is probably going to have good corporate governance standards in place. More so than the firm that doesn't bother to respond to customer complaints, or notes from the regulator.

I remember having a chat to a colleague working in a big investment bank. We were discussing mortgage payments. When told of my ethical fund arrangement, I got a small laugh in response. 'That's all very well but I like to make a return on my investments.' I'd chosen the funds on their performance as well as ethical criteria, I protested. But got nowhere. That discussion brought home the idea that many people consider high financial returns to be dependent on some intrinsically unethical activity. And don't want to know about it as long as there's 7 per cent gross at the end of each year.

Even the Church of England was found to invest in armaments firms.

But unethical firms are not good investments!

As the table below shows, this manufacturer of warplanes and defence contracts has seen its share price fall by 35 per cent. I don't think even the most risk-friendly soul would put money near tobacco these days and we can see why.

Name	Activity	Performance since May 1998
British Energy	Nuclear fuel	−63%
Diageo	Whisky, fast food	−40%
BAE Systems	Defence	−35%
British American Tobacco	Tobacco	−15%

BBC News | AMERICAS | Smokers' $145 billion court victory

Friday, 14 July 2000. 19:51 GMT 20:51 UK

In a landmark case in the United States, a Miami jury has ordered the tobacco industry to pay damages of $145 billion for knowingly causing smoking-related illnesses. Five US tobacco firms were found guilty last year of knowingly selling products that caused illnesses to users. One of the defendants, the Philip Morris tobacco company, said it would appeal against the decision. Alongside Philip Morris, the other companies named in the suit – RJ Reynolds Tobacco Co, Brown & Williamson Tobacco Corp, Lorillard Tobacco Co and Liggett Group Inc – have also settled cases in 50 US states, requiring them to pay an estimated $246 billion over a 25-year period.

'Lots of zeros, Lot of zeros,' was the comment from circuit court Judge Robert Kaye while reading the breakdown of damages against each of the defendants.

Companies that don't appeal to the right-minded now risk being left behind.

Of course, many firms with highly unpalatable activities turn huge profits. But there is a shunning of some brands that display an arrogance towards popular opinion. And firms that can point fairly to some societal benefit resulting from their activities – even if it is good employment practice – do seem to be doing rather well. Why else would firms want to be part of initiatives such as FTSE4Good or Heart of the City, where their social contribution is an essential for membership?

Capitalism, capitalism or, er, capitalism

Madam what can I get you today? I'd like a new economic world order please. Ah yes, here we are. Economic world orders. We have a choice of laissez faire or full-on brutish capitalism madam. Anything other than capitalism? I'm afraid not. OK I'll have to get one made.

Capital nows struts with confidence on a much wider stage. Trade restrictions lifted with China. In India, not Campa but Coca Colonization. As this new millennium gets into its stride, what is out there apart from capitalism? *Nada*. Our world is an open marketplace, with big business reaching into every village in every country, sometimes with fair and just practice for the employees and environment, often not.

We regulate our industries with national regulators. But the monopoly of capitalism. That's fine. What happens to a firm with monopoly power and no regulation? Exactly.

'In the last 20 years, there has been a significant increase in inequality in the pre-eminent capitalist economy, the United States. In 1981, the top 1 per cent of households owned a quarter of American wealth; by the late 1990s, that single percentage owned more than 38 per cent, higher than at any time since the 1920s.'

Niall Ferguson, Professor of Political and Financial History, Oxford University

So without real clout, there's a parade of toothless trade talks and unenforceable summit pledges on reducing debt and carbon dioxide emissions. Governments and Non Government

Organizations (people like Friends of the Earth, World Wildlife Fund) can only request change from the lords of the free market. I believe the task of insisting on fair play and reasonable regulation is down to us. That's right. Us with the spending power.

Consumers – you and I – aided by the occasional government or industry regulator, seem to be the only visible external conscience to the activities of lightly regulated trade. There are a lot of good businesses, with great labour relations and enlightened leadership: many of those have had excellent business results. However, when it comes to expansion, firms can expect few moral restrictions provided they offer regular employment to the local population. And no doubt firms push the agenda of max profit for least cost in all the ways a firm can – with direct consequences in terms of worker safety, benefits and well-being.

Given this backdrop, there's some evidence of change that merits some celebration. The capital that needs freedom and access can't multiply itself into profits without the know-how. Provided by you and me. Employee power. Not exactly the slogan of the moment. But as Kjell Nordstom and Jonas Ridderstråle, authors of *Funky Business* (FTPH, 2002) point out – 'Karl Marx was right . . . in a modern company 70 to 80 per cent of what people do is now done by way of their intellects.' Ownership of the means of production means what's behind our eyes and between our ears. Our brains.

Question If you needed something, badly, and were told you couldn't get it where you usually did – or if you could get it, but at twice the price – what would you do?

1. Try somewhere else.

2. Be nicer to the people who sell it hoping they'll change their minds.

This is the dilemma facing many big firms. And they're hedging their bets with a mixture of both.

1. Try somewhere else

Firms have increased overseas outsourcing and recruitment. Some believe that global capitalism is on a search for the cheapest and most docile labour. Hence women and child labour levels are increasing globally. The buying it elsewhere tactic is, for many firms, their best hope of retaining production and profitabilty levels. For many developing countries there's a chance to exploit western need for a low-cost resource – gaining infrastructure and foreign currency revenue. The challenge for those providing the resource is to exploit western need without labour being over-exploited in return. Clothing and sports shoe producer Nike has huge investments in developing countries – and found itself out of favour and facing a consumer campaign over its perceived exploitation of local workers. A BBC *Panorama* programme (October 2000) reported an conditions at production facilities in South East Asia. It didn't paint a favourable picture of Gap and Nike as global employers.

I used to like Gap – so what was all that about? (Doesn't it annoy you when the products you want to buy profit people you can't be sure of?)

2. **Be nicer to the people who sell it hoping they'll change their minds**

   The white charger I mentioned earlier – to the rescue. Firms no longer have cheap people a-plenty to line up as screen fodder. Which has led to some interesting developments. Offer cash, work, life balance and truth and the graduates might come to your milk-round presentation. Offer the same cash with a glossy brochure telling heroic stories of your CEO and watch the talent pool flow on to add to the strength of your competitors. **Trust is not a commodity**.

Moral leadership brand value

Showbiz has developed activist chic. Michael Douglas says no nukes. Susan Sarandon argues for the abolition of the death penalty in the USA. Richard Gere is a famous pro-Tibetan independence campaigner. Celebrities speak up and gain greater media coverage for the issues they choose to raise. They are shown as more caring, intelligent human beings. Good trade for the cause? Not always sure. Evidence of morality as good personal brand value material? Definitely.

When it comes to the corporate setting, the moral standing of senior players is becoming an important factor within overall brand strategy.

Leadership team qualities are a factor in determining overall brand strength. A young company seeking finance will be evaluated partially on the strength of its management team.

And brand – that alchemy of image and product promise – is becoming more and more important in determining overall corporate value. According to UK brand consultants Inter-brand Newel & Sorrell, a third of global wealth can be accounted for by brands.

So the leader morality factor is important. In some cases, for example, Richard Branson and Virgin, Anita Roddick and The Body Shop, and John T Chambers at Cisco, the leader is synonymous with the brand. We buy Sir Richard's financial services because he isn't a boring suit. We somehow feel he should sort out the Virgin Train services with the same chutzpah as he showed taking on British Airways over North American routes. Anita has crusaded tirelessly against animal testing and her sheer personal devotion to the cause makes us feel a little bit better about ourselves when buying The Body Shop facecream. John T. Chambers wants to rule the Internet/ telecoms equipment world from San José, and do it with integrity and honour and generosity. So:

- CEO change activist brand value? High.
- CEO no particular moral agenda no ability to handle change. Brand value? Low.

The CEO's character becomes an ingredient of the brand: intan-gible, laden with market value. And that's why leadership brand value is a highly market-sensitive valuation. So when Electric Henry (financial markets name for small investors) reads about the goodness or otherwise of corporate leaders, that will be a factor influencing their on-screen flutter. So any example of a leader of a publicly quoted company visibly demonstrating less than fabulous character is increasingly linked to company value. The moral leader is a brand strength, and the trend is increasing. There seems to be a connection between what the person stands for and trust in the product or service offered by the organization.

So the leader who is willing and able to demonstrate change activist capacity potentially has a source of competitive differentiation in the marketplace.

On the other hand, the leader who's a slimeball can also – undoubtedly – sell products. But perhaps only to other slimeballs. Just a thought.

Leaders have internal brand value too

Looking internally, there is also an internal brand value of leaders. Leaders who can articulate direction and create a structure within which people feel sufficiently valued to really contribute. The pay-off here is not so much PR but the abilty to recruit and retain the best people. The senior teams with poor leadership reputation risk low morale, higher employee defection and – worse than all that – becoming out of touch with the marketplace. Scary bosses get told what they want to hear (lies about what's really happening) so they can't take action until it's too late.

Industries are littered with tales of status-mad senior team leaders who really didn't do much for the self-esteem of their teams. A report in April/May 2000 into behaviour at a UK hospital showed that 'a culture of fear' had allowed a senior gynaecologist to botch hundreds of operations. He was clearly out of control, causing liver and kidney damage during routine surgery to hundreds of women. No one felt able to challenge him because he terrified, bullied and silenced the doctors and nurses working alongside him. The report spoke of 'failures in senior NHS management' and 'the old boys' network' and 'a climate of fear and retribution'. Police are expected to investigate the deaths of six patients.

Now this is perhaps an extreme case, but I suspect most of us have experienced a situation where the nearest manager wanted an ego stroke rather than the truth. Eventually we either confront or leave – neither making for a particularly happy workplace in the meantime. The character of the manager is a factor in making us, the employee, want to stay or go. And these days, with increasing skills shortages, many firms will want us as much as we want them.

Firms are beginning to realize that management loyalty to their staff is critical to retaining the best talent. As well as the share options, car payments, airmiles . . .

'A 10 000 aspirin job.'
Japanese term for executive responsibility

Case study: firms with activist ways

'The apparent lack of willingness by many in business to respond positively to the public's desire for corporate transparency is a real cause for concern.'
Extract from 'The Co-operative Bank Partnership Report 1999'

There is a case study (taken from *Working with Emotional Intelligence* by Daniel Goleman, (Bloomsbury, 1999) that illustrates the activist mindset at work, in a multinational corporate setting.

Levi Strauss employed sewing sub-contractors in Bangladesh, who were found to employ children. Human rights activists were rightly (in my view) angry that Levi used under-aged workers. After investigating, Levi found that if those children lost their jobs they would be forced to a level of poverty – and quite possibly be driven into prostitution. So what was the choice? Fire them and be able to say no we don't use child labour? Or carry on to ensure that at least they had an income?

Levi decided to do neither. They decided to keep paying the children their current wages, while they went to school full time. Then aged 14 – local working age – hire them back.

Now Levi ain't perfect. But as this incident shows, by having a social activist mindset, they were able to take their responsibilty seriously and come up with an option that seemed to be morally and financially correct. What do you think? Does knowing this make feel you more or less inclined to buy their jeans?

Change activism where you work

Each one of us lives on a spectrum of change fluency.

Translating from the natural world, there are some species that adapt, evolve, learn from external stimuli and diversify. And some that drive huge cars, eat baconburgers for lunch and ignore their employee welfare. There they are. Sitting alone, in a gleaming beamer, in a traffic jam inching towards extinction.

Given that there is business merit in being change fluent, able to take action based on values, what are the best ways to do it?

Well first of all change is more applicable in some parts of the business than others. Most organizations have some routine and generic things to do every day, just to keep things working. Operations management, and manufacturing environments, typically. Concerned with business as usual. In the baked bean production line baked beans keep being produced. With baked-in continuous improvement, obviously.

The production process remains fairly unchanged day in day out. Important to get right. Not requiring a huge level of change and therefore, if you're at organizational change beginner level, a comfortable place to live. If your working life has been spent in an operational background, there's a danger that although you know how to solve problems and keep things moving day to day, you might not be quite as nimble when it comes to handling projects or an organizational change programme.

In terms of the value that companies – rightly or wrongly – place on individual competency, there is a salary and career progression that is often linked to individual comfort with change.

Let's take another example, say from the IT/dot.com environment.

1. **The programmer** Comfortable as long as things stay constant. Has a clear role and a finite level of responsibility. Potentially a very good place to start being a change

activist, because company value = data in the digital age. However, influence at senior levels may take sometime.

2. **The project manager** Comfortable managing change. Has to negotiate responsibilities, budget and authority levels. Has potential to extend power and profile. Usually working within an overall IT programme – and can influence at senior levels in many cases.

3. **The programme manager or senior intrapreneur** Change fluent – potentially a change activist. Has to negotiate entire nature of business with major stakeholders. Able to redefine objectives to stay in line with changing market expectation. Usually heading organization or at board level – so definitely has opportunity to activate change.

Characteristics of 1 – comfortable with business as usual:

- becomes uncomfortable faced with change in routine or responsibility

- resistance to learning and development opening up to new ideas

- focus on short-term results

- boss or hierarchy focus – few stakeholders

- task orientation

- reactive work approach – I do as I'm told

- functional organization perspective, e.g. only deals with people in the same department

- limited sense of personal responsibility for organizational success

- sees other departments and the outside world as 'them and us'.

Characteristics of 2 – comfortable with change:

- fluency with change
- openness to learning and development
- able to justify the business investment in change
- focus on pleasing the client and customer
- task orientation
- deals with multiple stakeholders
- proactive work approach
- helps to broaden organizational perspective
- sense of personal responsibility
- creates interdepartmental coalitions.

Characteristics of 3 – change activist:

- passion for learning
- clarity on all kinds of investment
- identifies and builds coalition of diverse stakeholders
- expects high performance and success
- a pro-active work approach in terms of organizational and market perspective
- very strong sense of personal responsibility for outcomes.

Trust

'Trust is the driving force behind change. In today's business climate trust is losing the battle. Our corporations, one of our most important societal assets, seem to work against people trusting each other. Commercial enterprises are organised around a competitive paradigm which does not necessarily serve our long term common good. How do we start trusting ourselves to move from an old business paradigm which has made incredible technological progress but cannot carry us into the future? ... How can we trust ourselves to make the transition to sustainable technology that works on behalf of an integrated social, economic and environmental development?'

Michael Ray and John Renesch (eds), *The New Entrepreneurs*

Considering activist tools for business success brings me rather uneasily to this question of trust. Believe me, I'm not going to say activists have any extra trust genes, or that multi-issue coalitions are easily built. It's simply that at the moments when I have decided to take non-violent direct action, faced with the media, police et al. – those are the moments when I've had to trust absolutely in my fellow protesters. That no one would hit back when hit. That we would all maintain our dignity. That we would all make the same few points, clearly to camera before being bundled away. Absolute trust supports absolutely.

And in the business and organizational environment, given the upheavals and angst of constant change, I believe that trust is a core component of competitive advantage. Without it, there's no choice but contracts and checking and checking of checking. And on a human level, what would our workplace feel like without it? How would you cope if you felt untrusted, and unable to place trust in others. Hard, cold, lonely and in a place you'd want to leave? Probably. Because trust is our underlying contract with the world. It feeds and clothes our souls.

'Trust is as vital a form of social capital as money is a form of actual capital.'

Matt Ridley, *The Origins of Virtue*

Trust – benefits

	Lack of trust – costs	Importance in a time of change
Co-operation	Individual agendas	Improved teamwork
Knowledge sharing	Knowledge hoarding	Flexibility, learning power
Market shorthand for brand – I'll buy it because I trust the firm.	Market caution – will the thing work?	Competitive advantage
Low bureaucracy culture – deals done without checks	Higher cost of management checkers	Speed, openness and honesty
Risk taking, accept failure as part of learning	Lack of entrepreneurial energy, fear of change	Slower to learn from mistakes and seize new market opportunities

Do you build or destroy trust?

Do your actions match your words? Trust builder

Do you expect people to get things right? Trust builder

Do you hope that language in itself will create trust, e.g. do you call your colleagues 'team' but work with them as a hierarchy? Trust breaker

Are you impartial, or do you have favourites? What would that be?

Do you involve people and inform them even when there's bad news to share? Trust builder

Are you consistent, or do you change your mind and expect people to stay behind you? Trust breaker

Do you keep secrets – withhold information that could be shared? Trust breaker

Are you seen to be equitable – with pay rises etc? Trust builder

Do you take care of individual development, keep your training promises? Trust builder

(Adapted from *Bulletpoint Magazine*, January 1997)

What did you make of that? What would your colleagues say? This might be a pretty good 'to thine own self be true' audit, if you're up to it. What value do you put on trust? It might be worth while finding out.

Trust or dispute. Your call

The UK Advisory, Conciliation and Arbitration Service (ACAS) is called in as soon as there is a workplace dispute that turns into a legal dispute. It's a government body, set up for the purpose of resolving industrial conflicts, assisting employees against both their employers and their unions. It tries to agree a settlement between two parties in an employment dispute where legal proceedings have begun. Given that in 1999 they were called in to deal with 120,000 cases of unfair dismissal in the UK alone, they are well placed to advise on how to avoid a situation of extreme mistrust. Based on their years of impartial experience and business consultation, they publish an excellent overview as part of their 'Working Together Standard', which I reproduce here in full.

They begin by advising:

'Exchange information, pool ideas and share concerns with employees and their representatives and develop mutual trust.'

The subtext here, I guess, is, 'if you don't, you risk painful, expensive and public legal proceedings.'

Hazards of not sharing information, ideas and concerns: (source: ACAS):

- suspicion and distrust
- rumours and gossip
- wasting employees' knowledge, skills and ideas

- inefficiency

- dissatisfied customers.

And they have the following advice for employers. Don't forget this is UK-based guidance – some aspects will translate internationally, some won't.

The ACAS checklist – as an employer do you need to take action to improve the way you:

- provide employees with written statements of the main terms and conditions of employment together with grievance and disciplinary procedures?

- give employees up-to-date information about the organization and listen to what they have to say?

- use a variety of ways of sharing ideas and information – e.g. briefings, staff meetings, newsletters, e-mail, notice boards?

- communicate with all employees including part-timers, shift workers and those away from the workplace?

- make information available to employees and job candidates who have language difficulties, impaired vision or other disabilities?

- consult with trade unions and other employee representatives and individuals?

- work together with employees and their representatives?

So where does your firm stand on those?

On a lighter note, for yourself, here's a quick checklist. The aim is, the more you know yourself, the more you trust yourself.

Reality checklist

Look at the whole range of current projects and other stuff you're working on. Take one fairly important project. Look at the project objectives. Are they really the true objectives? What are you personally hoping to get from making it happen? And if you are honest what can you learn about your workplace trust levels from it?

I am working on this project in order to:

- create the impression of being busy
- genuinely improve our ways of working internally
- appear helpful to my boss who asked me to take it on
- gain new skills and development
- establish political credibility
- improve a product or service for our customers
- prove to my peers that I can do this big stuff
- get a promotion or bonus
- go on paid vacation. They never check on me!
- Other reasons – write all that you can think of.

All I'm suggesting is that it's very easy, as human beings, to believe our own hype. And as we believe the hype about how great we are, how indispensible, how personable – whatever

– I believe we risk leaving behind the person who learns, wants feedback, doesn't have a lot of face to lose. And leaving that person behind, in the world where feedback and flexibility and honour are increasingly rated, could be expensive. In lots of ways.

Cracks appear in the career veneer

The cliché of 1960/70/80s organizational man was that employees really did want the same life that the paternalistic organization wanted for them. Perhaps for some people that was and still is true. But it sounds like a somewhat covert contract to me.

There might not have been much else on offer on the psychological contract deli display. It was simply the way work was. Not an open-plan cafeteria, more a members' bar where no one needed to state the rules because, well, it was obvious. Today's exchange is potentially more explicit. Staying with the food analogy. Employee: 'Could I have free spirit but highly paid, to

Can we be a bit more honest with ourselves about why we do our jobs?

go please. Oh sorry, you just have the club abject subjugation and lifelong employment today. Thanks I'll pass.'

Imagine being able to say – to yourself – 'I want to achieve as much as I can while I'm here, as well as use this job to learn and move on to a brighter, more groovy and promising future. I'll stay for two years tops, and am OK with their lack of strategic follow-through and poor IT in the meantime.'

Take my friend and what she says about her current job as a sales manager. 'For a long time I didn't exactly lie about why I worked there, but I wasn't exactly truthful either. The fact was, I didn't really know what I wanted to do; I knew that I needed to earn money, and they pay well. So I came up with this very believable interview act about my lifelong admiration of the management style of this firm. And they hired me. Now I feel like a big fraud.'

Traditionally, trading organizations haven't really needed to care about issues such as emotional employee allegiance. On the basis of supply and demand. One legacy is a lack of language when it comes to truthful debate about why we are at work. At an extreme, some organizations have taboos about us declaring our true motivations.

There are some conversation topics that that work less well during your first week. 'I'm here for the share option benefits.' 'I came because you offer more training than the other firms in this town.' 'I work as VP Finance because I live in that apartment over there and I want to walk to work.'

Do any of us say that? Nope. It's 'I really admire your long history of producing world-class office supplies and I knew from childhood my destiny was to manage your PC helpdesk.' Mmm. Let's see. Let's build our financial and professional future on a big fat lie. How does that feel? Not great actually.

And it isn't even necessary. As an activist I learned very quickly that honesty about my own motivation for being involved in the campaign was absolutely essential. Because anything less than 100 per cent commitment would be immediately visible as soon as the going got tough (why did Carmel go shopping when the police arrived?).

The activist tool of being honest about what motivates us could be really useful. We fear that by removing the veneer of total allegiance we'll become something less attractive to our firms, and be marked at appraisal time as visibly different. We'll become

Airing true views about why you want to do your job in an honest way doesn't mean you'll view your in-tray diffrently, much less do your job badly.

vulnerable through our huge disloyalty. Yet how many times have you been on a team-building offsite event where, after some insight into the range of motivations present in the same team, you heard people saying: 'Oh my gosh, I didn't realize you felt the same way'? My experience has been that most fast com leaders really want honest feedback from their people as part of the job – not at the exit interview. But I suspect your own low self-esteem is as much to blame as those bad employers out there.

Who wrote the rule saying when you sign the contract of employment you waive all rights to question company objectives? Or to want to trade your time and expertise quite honestly just for cash? The psychological contract of contractors is judged to be mercenary, less loyal. Perhaps in earlier times that was true. Perhaps in the army it's still true. But perhaps we're all mercenaries until we're able to find a place where we can act on our values and be given space to act and grow. Then we become attached by more than the money.

'What's the sense in getting rich if you just stare at the ticker tape all day.'

Warren Buffett

It's OK to recognize that we want to achieve more than just the current set of project objectives. Surely it's a little bit healthier to understand ourselves and be honest with ourselves. In an ideal environment wouldn't it be a good thing if the project manager stood up at the definition meeting and said:

'This project is going to build some software which will knock the pants off our CRM competitors. It's fantastic, with wonderful functionality and I'm going to make sure that this company gets it sooner rather than later. And that we don't break the bank getting it. Also I've never been to Hong Kong, except for a stopover two years ago, so ladies and gentlemen. I'm going to be based there for the second month of the roll-out and do the relationship management task with our clients in Asia. The reasons why that is good for the company are explained in this document 'Stuart@hongkong'. And in the course of this project I intend to develop some fantastic account management skills, which I think this company needs more of. Thank you, and I look forward to working with each and every one of you.'

What would that be like? What would be the upside or downside for organizations?

Value-based leadership and change honesty create the next level of success fluency for business.

Being part of a high-performance team has been described as participants being truly honest with themselves and other members of the team about the motivation for achieving the team objectives. That honesty strips away the layers of politicking, ego positioning and self-protection, which we have seen to be expensive and time-consuming.

The next page of business history is going to rely on that explicit link. Equals next page business fluency. The next page is full of stories of companies who seek out social entrepreneurs, pensions activists, environmentalists as employees and advisers, because those people will argue for ethical strategies, social contribution as well as shareholder value. Thereby creating a more honest link with more consumers and investors. Watch this space.

Corporate allegience is optional. And at the most shallow level, for sale. Pay me well and I will applaud your colourful powerpoints. As soon as a better paid job comes up, I'm off. At the deepest level, individual integrity, and a truthful connection to the aims and objectives of the organization, is the fuel that works beyond golden handcuffs, pension plans and a nice waterfall in the atrium. As a boss, honesty towards stakeholders and clarity with your employees about what you, as a fallible human, are expecting to happen will bring tangible rewards to your company, for getting it right.

I have the right to disagree. Don't I?

It was summer 1982. I was trying (with a number of other very determined women) to stop first-strike nuclear missiles being stationed at the RAF base at Greenham Common in Berkshire. Which is about 50 miles west of London, England.

Asking the very decent and civil police of the local town not to drag peaceful protesters away was met with: 'I'm only carrying out instructions, love, I don't make the rules.' 'But do you agree with the rules?' Silence. 'Are you happy that you live four miles from a nuclear target you had no say about.' Silence. 'Do you mind if we sing?' Ill-judged wrong footing tactic. Silence. 'Sorry love, I have to tell you that you are not obliged to say anything but that anything you do say will be taken down and may be used in evidence against you. I am arresting you for blah blah blah.'

That day I realized that police obey orders first and think about them later. It struck a chord. It was the same as my bosses in the investment bank (an earlier and quite different career). Same, I imagine, as the middle managers of Global Utility Inc. There's danger in being off-message about your firm. Almost treason to pull the brand into any mire publicly. How does it work where you are?

I want those nice human rights people to be invited into many of the offices I've have worked in. Where we sat behind our PCs and drank coffee and wrote budget spreadsheets and had our dreams implode by the side of our keyboards. Having any kind of outspokenness or personality at work was a definite career-limiting factor. We sat in the pub afterwards and if we could still bear to face the same faces, spoke about our job and the weird thing is that the PR lived on even after we'd left the office building. We still say the things that should be said – but only to ourselves. In the shower. Those organizations that had very nice colours on the annual report and only grey male faces on the board. No nice colours allowed in the board meetings. Only in the 'Smile, It's the Company Bullshit Magazine' – now available on the Web. Official smiling for the company websites is big business.

This leads to problems.

We need honest dissent at work – dialogue aimed at raising problems in order to fix them. I'm not talking about telling the nearest journalist how to find a nasty angle on your firm's less than perfect ways. I'm saying that we need debate **We need honest dissent at work.** and dialogue to help push the argument about the best way to do business on to a better place.

That example – did you know that loads of Internet banking call centres allocate bathroom passes to the people who staff their phone lines? Wow. There's progress for you.

Stay loyal or be sacked

BBC staff had been told to stay loyal or be sacked according to an article by John Arlidge in the *Observer* (23 April 2000). Apparently the new boss has told 'some of the best known names in British broadcasting' that they could be fired if their criticism of the BBC extends beyond the walls of their offices in London. In response, one senior broadcaster said: 'The BBC is more than a bloody brand. It is an essential part of British life. If people honestly feel things are going wrong, they should be able to say it without worrying a P45 [meaning a termination notice] will land on their desk.'

Implicit in that is that if the BBC were simply a brand of soap powder or fizzy drink, then employees would have to be silent for fear of endangering the brand image. And that would be OK.

In more radical moments I think that capitalism seeks docile and malleable workers in order to preserve maximum profit and minimum cost. And given that an employee's point of view can't always be exactly where the company spin doctors want it to be. OK chaps, the agenda today is let's just stop any free thinking anywhere.

"I want the public to think of us as 'The Company With A Heart.' But I want you to think of us as the company that will chew you up, spit you out and smear you into the carpet if you screw up.'

Call centre workers. Broadcasters. Scared to take an extra trip to the bathroom or speak out publicly. The reason we don't see articles about the call centre workers presumably is market value. Aren't call centre workers two a penny? Aren't they cheap labour, not needing specialist skills, can use phone and PC and will be good customer fodder after only a few weeks' training? Therefore will accept rules, which are at least inconvenient and to most people unreasonable. Broadcasters, on the other hand, have some personal brand and do matter.

By the way – an explanation of the new BBC code on criticism was published. A BBC source said:

'We are competing in a more and more competitive world, where image matters. We need to look united and profes-sional.'

Observer, 23 April 2000

So there we are then. I look forward to the BBC repositioning itself alongside Proctor & Gamble and Microsoft as big brands with big smiling consensed to death managers, wondering what's safe to say.

Many organizations have a feedback tool called 360 degrees (which means inviting peers and bosses and your team and lots of others in the office to tell you honestly how you're doing) linked to performance management. Some managers insist on being able to see the feedback from work peer to work peer – but won't personally participate in the scheme themselves. By the way, how free are you to give honest feedback to the people who pay you? Feedback – rich firms/teams/individuals tend to be successful because learning happens with feedback.

Firms that manage by relationship

How can you tell if your workplace runs on fear?	Circle which is most true for you	If you said yes, this is what might be happening
Lots of emphasis on looking after client/customer	Yes that's true Not really	Service orientation – market led
Lots of projects, as well as regular jobs. Prospects are usually quite cool	Yes there are Not many of them	Flexibility towards change, spontaneous action. Matrix organizations likely
Global, technology friendly	Yes Nope	Future mindset
You work in a team and rely as on others to help out – genuinely	Yes Not here. It's dog eat dog	Teamwork perceived key to performance
There's usually a good debate before big decisions	Yes Not true	Dissent friendly – likely to result in decisions backed by those about to do the work
Your business card has your name, job description, address and mobile on it	Yes it does No it doesn't	Roles are clear, good customer focus and I may work 24/7
The boss encourages a chat, and seems OK	That's right Not true	Informal hierarchy; employees valued
Some suppliers usually come along to the company do	Yes of course Why should they?	Integrated process links; Concept of stakeholder value emerging
Share, save or employee option scheme	Yes that's true Nope	Potential for inclusive ownership
Recognized trainee development plan	Yep We don't bother	Employees seen as important asset

Places run on trust. The future, maybe...

There is a desire to make money – or meet the organization's goals and keep growing in quality, as well as contributing to society and retaining good people.

How can you tell?	Circle which is most true for you	If you said yes, this is what might be happening	Business benefits
You plan your next project with customers, suppliers and the community in mind – and get feedback on your product from them	Yes I do No I don't	Diverse feedback – improved alignment	Improved relationship and loyalty. Integrated process means faster handovers. Earlier visibility of problems, enabling fast and less expensive fix
You feel a powerful connection with your work colleagues	Yes Not many of them	Energy, openness	Team speed of reaction, elegant team solutions
Your boss helps with what you're doing	Yes, thank goodness No way	Sense of value – leading to improved commitment and desire to stay	Lower attrition rates
You expect to get challenged on the quality of what you do	Yes Not me	Continuous learning and stimulation	Stretch and growth
The emphasis is on learning and getting to be 'the best' through making mistakes and improving	Yes it is Not true	Risk taking, innovation	Faster cycle times, creative market edge

How can you tell?	Circle which is most true for you	If you said yes, this is what might be happening	Business benefits
Clients expect integrity and commitment from you	Yes they do. You bet! Not true. How sad.	Performance becomes a matter of personal pride and honour	Dedicated and bespoke performance
The work gives you a chance to really express what you care about	That's right Not true	Sense of fulfilment, being energized	Clients sense the commitment and want more
Your business card has just your name, e-mail and mobile on it	Yes No	It's what you contribute that matters	Easy to remember!
The senior team encourages community involvement	Yes that's true Nope	Sense of wider societal connection and responsiveness.	Opening your heart and living beyond the bottom line
You're a part owner of the firm	Yep No	Longer-term perspective and commitment	Responsibility, a chance of big dividend payouts and pride

03

chapter three

practical activism – here's how

social activists: faster and smarter than suits?

FOR CAMPAIGNS to succeed, the activist has to be faster and smarter than the institution or individual being challenged. Activists have fewer material resources – certainly in relation to big corporations. So the advantage has to come from inner, rather than outer resources, for example outrageous creativity, the ability to trust and support each other and simple, quiet bravery when it comes to the event.

GLASBERGEN

"Let's form a committee to create a task force to develop a team to determine the fastest way to deal with the problem."

The arrogance of some big firms has also been a huge asset to activists! Activist campaigns have won some notable victories – against the odds. Taking on the might of oil multinationals to defend indigenous people and the environment, tackling the GM food producers, to name but two.

Can business leaders learn anything from that genuine passion and activist approach? If you were, say, director of an IT consultancy, would doing the right thing, as much as the most profitable thing, benefit your employees, customers and the people who choose to invest in your firm? Your life is full of the case studies.

Do you know anyone who works in a place where egos fly unbounded? Where there is perhaps too much bureaucracy? Where e-mail is the easier alternative to sorting it out here and now? Well, those places do not make happy employees. Unhappy employees don't usually thrill customers.

So perhaps those big old companies can be helped to understand and emulate best activist techniques. And do so with a moral soul as well.

Dinosaurs missed out on survival. Birds survived. Andersen shredded their reputation along with those guilt disclosing Enron files. Firms with visibly ethical leaders survive economic downturn. Firms without an ethically buyable board deserve a past-tense existence. Enough writers have commented on Darwin and the evolution of business.

Now its time to check out your own situation. Is your desk in a cosy niche of a big firm? How long does it take to get a decision from your senior managers? Longer than it takes two people to read a page on e-mail? OK, you may be aboard a dinosaur.

Change activism is eyes wide open looking at your desk in the context of what you want to achieve with your life. Are you dealing with it?

If this is the case, what can you do? If you don't want things to move quickly – fine. You're well placed. If, however, you feel that life is to be relished and cherished and made the most of – then you need to help change your firm or move on. This exercise might help you make up your mind.

Exercise

Are you onboard the next Enron?

Answer true/false on the following questions.:

1. I can be honest and open about the contents of my job with anyone. True/False

2. My firm spends more than it earns (check this via the friendly local accountant, the annual results, and/or common sense). True/False

3. My CEO/Managing Director is accessible and encourages honest questions from the staff. True/False

4. If I disagree with a board-level decision, I am able to say what I feel. True/False

5. Our leaders ensure our financial accounting system is open to scrutiny by everyone in the organization. True/False

6. I can dissent without fear of retribution. True/False

7. My bonus is dependent on a wide range of measures, some financial, some team performance, some people related. True/False

8. If someone in the team takes short cuts (e.g. moves figures around to make the budget work) we have a way of making sure it gets picked up and stopped. True/False

9. My boss is keen to share accurate data on our performance with other departments. True/False

10. We have a corporate governance statement which is applied to our day-to-day actions. True/False

If you tick true more than four times, please consider the following action:

- Copy the page and discuss with your team – what causes things to work? What could you do more of internally?

- Copy the page and discuss with your customers – what more could you do to make them proud to deal with you?

- Copy the page and discuss with your senior team – what can you all decide to do to improve on this good stuff?

The activist sees life from a more focused viewpoint. There's an urgency to each day. The underdogs. The best companies try to make employees feel they have a stake and some ability to direct the details of their job. Right now looking at the great and the good of commerce – and consolidation means the *Fortune* Top 20 is full of multimultinationals, many of them have tried to sow the seeds of small firms thinking. Before he retired, Jack Welsh, CEO at GE, instructed his team to 'destroy your process' before someone else does. British Telecom breaking itself up into smaller, e-strategic business units hoping they'll reach the customer niche more effectively. Wonder how they'll recreate that small, clear, determined–about–life buzz again.

Activists are juiced on values. And that gives a huge boost to performance. When you wake up in the morning and want to go out in the rain and get the bus, because the work waiting for you when you get there gladdens your heart, reflects the values you hold dear. Values are the fuel for our careers and our life achievements. Values – the things that are most important to you. If your job doesn't rotate around them, you will start to rotate around something that allows you to escape. A drink, a busy hobby, or TV. Are you working on something that means a lot or a little to you right now?

Values sometimes seems to be a laden term? I contend that values are essentially neutral. You can have high moral values, or low moral values. The words denote a hierarchy. But let's just consider the wider picture.

When one person is asked – what is important to you? – they might reply – the values I live my life by: honesty, freedom, justice and creating a loving homelife.

When asked to rank them in order of importance, they might place honesty first. When asked why, they might say that they prize honesty because it's the foundation for the things they want to achieve. When asked for an example, they might say, well, if I feel that I can be completely honest with my friends and colleagues at work, I am happier, more relaxed. I feel that honesty is the cornerstone of my life. Honest business is good business and I can feel at peace with myself.

Ask another person. What is important in your life, OK, financial security, a nice house, big car, at least two international vacations per year. What is most important? Oh, easily money because then I can do what I want. If I have money then I feel good about myself and have fun. I enjoy living the high life. So money is very important to me.

Both these people live by their personal values. The first person wants to ensure that s/he lives a life of honesty. The second is guided by financial success. Who's to say right and wrong without understanding context? There's certainly cause and effect in terms of building everything around money at the expense of relationships or societal contribution. But who can judge that choice? In *The Power of Ethical Management* (Vermillion, 2000), Peale and Blanchard say that working for money alone is like playing tennis only to see the scoreboard.

Would being a materialistic person mean you have fewer friends? Would dedicating yourself to helping others make you more popular? Well it just isn't as simple as that. Our life choices are guided by the often invisible steer of our values. And we create change with greater or lesser urgency depending on the prominence we give to certain values. I know some great investment bankers who work full on for money. That's their number one. Why? Because they want a life without personal debt, and to give their kids a better home life than they were able to have.

And I know some social activists who live for personal growth and development and have become so inwardly focused that they don't know how to give to others at all on a one-to-one level.

One suggestion on values and balance comes from the Life Orientations organization, which over 30 years has developed a personal development framework through understanding basic personality types and preferences. It suggests that any strength, carried to extreme, becomes a weakness. So avoid being so supportive that your co-team leader can't get a word in edgeways. The route away from dysfunction is to value diverse values and to assess what is most important to you.

Exercise

What is most important to you?

Write down the things that are most important to you right now.

And try to put them in a ranked order – 1 to 10.

Then ask yourself if I could have 1 but not 2, which would I choose? If you could have freedom, but not money, which would you choose? Fun but not time with your family, which would you choose? Check out your first guesses.

Do this exercise with someone who knows you. Ask for their views.

Is there anything more important than finding out the values that can potentially fuel all you do?

The toolkit for change

After considering my own activist experience, and learning about a number of other campaigns, it became apparent that a core set of skills and attributes form a common foundation when organizing for non-violent social change. I have pulled them together into a change activist toolkit.

The toolkit – to be found in successful activist campaigns:

1. clarity of objective
2. motivation and motivational leadership
3. trust and care – emotional intelligence
4. inclusive ways of working
5. communication
6. sense of self-esteem and worth in the world
7. physical stamina.

One person who has demonstrated each of these is A. John Bird, interviewed here.

Change activists

Interview – A. John Bird, Founder, *The Big Issue*

CM *Carmel McConnell (interviewer)*
AJB A. John Bird (interviewee)

CM *How did you become an activist – what made you start* The Big Issue?

AJB Gordon Roddick of The Body Shop saw a successful street magazine in the US and thought – we could do that in London and he asked me to start it up in the UK. I asked him to fund the magazine that homeless people could sell and retain a high percentage of the cover price. He gave that help and The Body Shop allowed vendors to sell outside their premises. We took one idea – one product if you like – and made it work in Sydney, in London, in Johannesburg, in Manchester and have helped hundreds of thousands of people in transition over ten years. And we keep growing.

CM *What is your biggest need now and your biggest cause for pride?*

AJB My big challenge now? I want to demonstrate the power of workable solutions – practical projects. And blueprint them.

I want to be a force for change involving business and the public sector and to create completely new forms of investment. For example, a social bank that will provide start up capital to recycling businesses, community resources. And make it work.

CM *Do you see yourself as a kind of social broker then?*

AJB Yes – if you mean I help business and the community work together and challenge the separation of social and business.

CM *What is your advice for people who feel they would like to contribute to society, but don't know how?*

AJB Don't judge. And remake yourself if you are not happy. Use all the skills you have – you can do something. Think about what you would like to see done and ask yourself – what are you prepared to do?

Underneath the veneer of civilization – our day to day working lives – there is a whole world of people who do need all of us to care. For example there is a woman in her sixties who sleeps in the doorway two doors away from this café – I know that she had children, she had a mental illness and that at one stage she just walked out of her home. Her family will have tried to help but couldn't. Now there may be extra problems there I don't know – what I do know is that woman does get flashbacks of her earlier life – who knows she may even remember that she has had a family – and sometimes when I walk past here in the evening she is crying. Now I just think we have to do something about it.

And I think that for your readers it is in your self interest to be a 30-year-old professional fighting for good elderly provision – good resthomes, good facilities. Change is always about mutual self-interest. When you ask yourself what am I getting out of this, there has to be some pay-off for each one of us helping to solve societies problems. There is going to be a net gain for the young professional who is able to consider these things as part of life. We need more people buying into the well-being of society because it is our well-being.

CM *What changes do you feel need to take place within the business world to address social issues?*

AJB We are in the foothills of social change with the involvement of business – and people like you and me are going to take this to the top of the Himalayas. I want to create awareness that funding social issues is good for shareholders, good for employees as well as good for the people who get help at the end of it. I am very involved with the business community helping people recognize the mutual benefits of solving the problems of society.

CM *What skills do you feel you have which have enabled you to be so successful?*

AJB I have tried to bring the social issues of homelessness to life through parables and stories.

It is essential if you want to reach people to put things in clear, accessible language. You can have all the knowledge in the world – what is important is to reach people in terms of their perception.

I know that I can reach people with my message in a way that connects to their emotion. In a room people end up saying what do you want me to do John! Then, when I am on a high, looking around and not quite knowing what to do next, that is when people like Sarah (my executive assistant) are absolutely vital to provide practical next steps for people. There has to be both if you want to bring about change – the passionate connection with something big and next day something practical you can do about it.

And I am full time on this. Talking to people working and wondering how we can sort our society out so that we do support those of us who end up disadvantaged or dispossessed. It's my life.

CM *Do you see business changing?*

AJB Definitely. I think business is evolving from where it is right now where it is simply about profits to what I call sexy profits based on sexy performance – which means you can strengthen the bottom line by community involvement, environmental action. The real bottom line is profit and sustainability. For example say you make 10 per cent profit but a quarter of that you have to spend on recruitment because you haven't created an environment where people want to stay. That is not sexy profit or sexy performance. Another example is the fact that at the Big Issue offices we spend quite a lot of money keeping the bathrooms in really good condition – now I don't often know how that money gets spent but I do know that if we stopped spending it there would be a subtle message to every employee who uses the bathroom – you are not really valued. So I think that business is going to have to adapt because as some firms do get those strengthened bottom lines – which we as consumers are getting more anxious about by the way – then there will be a real movement towards cultural and social echoes as part of the business agenda.

CM *What is the ideal outcome of the Big Issue campaign? What help do you need from the business community which will form the mass readership of Change Activist?*

AJB I want to end the situation where, if a person does lose their home or have circumstances that force them to become homeless, the welfare system pushes them down further causing them to lose self esteem. It is expensive to keep people down there. It is much better if people feel powerful enough to take decisions at personal level. When people have to ask for state help I want that experience to be like a trampoline to boost them right back up to feeling good about themselves – rather than feeling they've hit a swamp. So you lost your home and you have nothing. Fantastic – you have nothing to lose. What do you really want to do? Out of this could come your great opportunity to remake yourself.

By the way, I remade myself. But that's another story!

You have to fare well on welfare in order to say farewell to welfare. So we at the Big Issue are doing that – giving people pride – and we link closely to lots of agencies which offer people on the streets a range of development, urgent support using counsellors. We believe people are capable of huge transition that has been our experience.

Making activist skills work for you

The skills needed to make campaigns work are not new. You have probably got a combination of them in your organization already. The challenge is to develop activist capacity, based on a wide enough coalition of common purpose, within an environment where risk-taking and innovation are seen as critical to learning. Not reasons to resign. For leaders, the critical difference between transformation and being just another player is the deployment of a team with a wide enough portfolio of skills.

A change programme is one that seeks to make significant improvement in the organization, be that process or technology or culture. The best change efforts integrate all key elements – for example there's little point talking about the new customer-focused culture if the logistics constantly fail to deliver products when the customer needs them.

In this next section we will evaluate a few elements of the activist skillset, to understand each skill in detail and explore its potential application in your life. Can these skills be used to accelerate change in your organization? What about wanting to make changes in your career path? Your life?

Ability to think of the wider context

Taking action that results in real improvement in people's lives. OK, quick management translation for all you jargon-mongers out there. 'We need people who can see the big picture (not the Guggenheim by the way), who have helicopter perspective, who demonstrate thinking outside the box.' OK, it's over now!

What is this about? Thinking of the wider context is a mindset as well as a skill. It allows connection of thoughts and experience to a greater whole. There's the old story of the two people who were laying bricks in a wall. When asked, one bricklayer said his job was to make a good wall. The other guy said he was building a cathedral. Both are true. According to neurophysiologist Karl Pribram at Stanford University, 'the brain is a hologram interpreting the holographic universe.' A sense of perspective and compassionate detachment for the self is a critical activist skill. So let's take one example.

You are studying. Evenings and some weekends you work in a restaurant. Your head tells you this is good because the money helps you and you get skills you can always use. Also while working you can't spend money, right? Your heart is a little heavy because some customers don't appreciate the waiter even though it's an important job. The status sometimes feels lower than you would like.

Example **a)** Joe with an ability to think of the wider context

Example **b)** Joe's friend Matt with no ability to think of the wider context

a) Joe works in the restaurant three nights a week and earns $50. He is studying architecture. While working in the restaurant he wonders how the ambience is impacted by the design – for example, are customers in one corner happier than those in another? The ceilings are low – do people feel they can hear each other speaking when the restaurant is full? He asks the boss to add a question on the design of the place to the regular happy sheet (customer service form). Joe learns that the people who sit in quiet areas of the restaurant are more likely to say they will return. The boss is interested in this and Joe is hired to assess how soundproofing might work. Two months later the boss loves his report, Joe gets hired to work on plans and project manage the restaurent soundproofing improvements with a local firm of architects. He works one evening and Saturday and earns $200. So by thinking of a context wider than checking the pizza topping to the customer order, Joe benefits. He considers what makes the restaurant work as a whole. Wonders what might change. Asks questions. Takes action. And yes, Joe got hired for summer work with the local architects and five years later is a very happy junior partner in the firm.

b) Matt works the restaurant three nights a week and earns $50. He is studying business. While working he wonders how long it will be before the end of his shift and when he can meet his friends. He stays at the restaurant for six months on the same pay and gets an OK, but not great, reference from the boss. He finds Joe a bit too enthusiastic. They lose touch over time.

So let's consider you and the ability to think of the wider context. Very quickly run through these questions with me.

Quiz

Am I a big picture person . . .?

Answer the following questions, then use a green highlighter to mark areas where there seems to be a lot of energy or enthusiasm. Then use another colour highlighter to mark out any gaps.

Question	Answer
My job right now is	
My job is important to the firm/organization I work for because	

▶

Question	Answer
My firm/organization is important because it provides (describe service or product and describe customers or community being served)	
My work is important to the success of where I work because	
I understand what my boss does. It is	
I could step into my boss's job any time. True, false or maybe?	
This is my one line statement about how this firm/organization could become a much more successful place	

Question	Answer
This is what I could contribute to making that happen	
These are the three main reasons I am scared to do it	
And this is why I really would like to do something	
Who could help me do it?	
I value myself. What evidence?	

▶

Who will I talk to today, about
this idea on how to improve how
we do things round here

What does the page look like now you have highlighted the different responses? One colour? Lots? The trick now is to use some of the energy from some of the more fabulous areas to hit the gaps.

What are your priorities?

How will you take this forward?

What surprised you?

Date your answers – it might be useful to consider what changes over time. Hopefully you feel that your job is part of the landscape of your life, not all of it.

How useful in business is that? Every firm and organization needs the commitment and input of employees and partners. Being able to see the wider context of where you work and what you do is perhaps not something you have been used to doing. It takes a little practice and imagination to get above the stuff you do day to day – or the thoughts you have been used to thinking. But this first activist skill is really important on the trip to thine own self be true. Seeing your life in context means you see your life as part of a changing, malleable world. And you are the one who makes the changes happen.

How to develop those skills

Developing a sense of the wider context is not really too difficult. For starters, ask your family or a best friend what they think you do for a living. What do they actually think you do? Some members of my family still think I sell refrigerators in Italy. (I worked as a consultant for a home appliances company and my sister told them the name of the firm. Now when I go home there is always one cousin who wants to know how I am getting on with those freezers!)

Going back to you – time to do some research. Read one news story – local or international. Find out more about it. Be brave and ring the local TV station and ask who did the story. Or look on the Web. Or ask people what they understand. When you've identified a little more on the story, work out why it happened. What might have led up to it. What might come next.

Now take a business story. Yes I know it isn't quite as groovy. Pick one firm – maybe one like yours. Find out as much as you can about it. What is it doing? Who owns it? What problems or issues are they dealing with? What has been going on this year? Now, what's your view on what should happen. Why? What's going on in terms of customers – more or less happy? What about the competition? What would you do if the company belonged to you? Find out, and find someone to talk about it. If you find the financial side interesting, talk to the

finance people in your firm. Just get a good grasp of one story
– from the widest possible perspective. When you can understand the story overall it's much easier to identify key issues.

Now look at yourself, your desk or wherever, in a similar type
of company. From where you now sit, what might happen
next? What can you forecast, contribute to, comment on?
What action might it be wise to take? If you were a financial
journalist commentating on your company, what would you
advise someone in your job to do? Learn new skills? Go have
lunch with the head of e-business? Work out why the
competitors sell more in more territories than you do. Having
a sense of the wider context gives you real decision-making
power. And like every good soap opera, the more you get
hooked on the storyline, the better it gets.

Make decisions quickly and act quickly

Oh, the heady buzz of management. Preparing and reviewing
budgets. Taking notes. Turning up every day for your e-mails.
Filing.

There's a kind of commerce-based coma that can come over
us in the workplace. Doing the same kind of tasks on a regular
basis – even creative ones – can become a kind of physical
drone. And it can result in near permanent patheticness that
can seep into your whole life. When I worked in a big organization I was given objectives and a six-month period in
which to achieve them. Can you imagine how slow that felt
compared to the activists getting together on a Sunday night
to plan a media event on Tuesday! Slow objectives – do them

slowly because that's all they expect – have a habit of seeping into life. Slowly plan to leave this job. Slowly plan to do something more interesting. Personal change becomes infected by the snailpace of corporate change. And trust me – YOU CAN DO IT FASTER!!!

We hear about analysis paralysis – people who have to read one more report or analyze one more spreadsheet before recommending a course of action. You've probably worked with people who have existed one level ahead of their potted plant in terms of dynamism, tucked into that corner of the IT department. Sitting in that nice out-of-the-way office doing the accounts.

Doing nothing but paperwork and reports and attending the odd meeting about not much, causes a hugely reduced comfort zone for action. So the first time you try something other than writing reports – for example, doing that presentation – it's heartstoppingly out of your comfort zone. You do it, live, learn something and, guess

Don't lose the muscle in your head by accepting a job without challenge. The easy life leads to fewer options.

what, doing the next one is almost inside your comfort zone.

Like agoraphobia, management by repetition gives rise to sheer terror at the thought of a friendly chat with someone very senior. The worse stomach-ache you ever had on the morning of a meeting with very important clients.

The change activist difference is to keep on pushing your daily comfort zone into action. I'm not advocating that you become a one-woman (or one-man) frenzy of useless activity – simply

that if your job doesn't require action – which takes some of your courage and wit and determination to achieve – then it's quite possible that you haven't got a job worth doing.

And I just don't hold much patience with people who claim their job is great because they haven't got that much to do. On one level, there's an element of fraud – and no one feels great about being one of those. On another it's just like the person who claims staying in bed all day is so relaxing. Until they lose the use of the muscles in their legs. Don't lose the muscle in your head by accepting a job without challenge. The easy life leads to fewer options.

And another thing. Slow decisions are like no decisions in the fast-track areas of business today. Let's move ahead on this – yes, great. Can we all meet in three months? Fine. Message received – this is not important. Can we meet early next week with progress? Yes? This is happening. You might have heard the saying 'justice delayed is justice denied'. Try 'action delayed is idea just died'.

Providing you have all the building blocks in place – change has to be fast change. Or else we are back to commerce-induced coma. Pass me a pillow, I think there's room next to the keyboard. My boss is going check my objectives progress, sometime next winter.

Look at the timescale for decision-making where you work. Change activism is about speed – speed of thought, speed of decision, speed of action. Here's an example.

One afternoon at Greenham Common, we made a decision to gain publicity for the campaign, in the heart of London. We figured the City – as the centre of financial transactions funding arms development – would be a good place. And we wanted to make the point that the City is not above the arms trade just because it has an image of respectability. We wanted to do something that would be effective, peaceful and would allow us to state our case with good publicity. So we decided that a stop-the-traffic event would be best. We agreed that any emergency service vehicles would be able to get through – and let the authorities know that in advance. (I believe they re-routed ambulances.) One of the hard things about taking non-violent action is that it does undoubtedly cause inconvenience and that has to be managed, to keep public support. In our quest to make sure nuclear war didn't happen we felt our task was to get maximum public awareness before it was too late.

So on a bright Tuesday morning we decided to lie down on the crosswalks on the five main roads around Bank station – right in the heart of London's financial services district. It was a complex task – we figured that we needed over 200 people to make it work. Ten per each one of the five crossings, in short shifts, for 30 minutes. We got there, took a deep breath and some of us laid down in front of the traffic, some gave out leaflets explaining what we were doing. After 30 minutes we stopped. And the police arrested only a few of us because the traffic couldn't get through.

We did stop the City of London for a while – that was the time before e-mail and quite a few of the roads were full of couriers. One motorcyclist ran over a crossing injuring three women in the process. We did get publicity and showed that we were prepared to take our protest to more locations.

One thing that surprised journalists was that we decided on the action on Sunday night, did it on Tuesday, had global news coverage by Wednesday. That was one of our secrets. How did we do it? Well this happened in April and about 30 of us had lived outdoors for most of the winter together. We had learned to trust and respect each other for our individual skills. We were able to gather information from a very focused network of experts. We had friends and supporters in almost every profession – ok, I admit perhaps not many soldiers or nuclear scientists – and our speed was unbelievable.

Going back to the workplace – commerce-induced coma attacks not only individuals but whole organizations. And that's dangerous in a world where speed to market is competitive advantage. Decision-making and action – getting there before your competitor. Or getting the paper out before some new recruit two floors down who has just decided he wants your job . . .

In the technology economy, expect your firm to launch software, ideas, marketing strategy in minimum time. And no more luxury of sequential planning. The critical path plan shows everything in parallel. So – the pressure and reward require that you share information, have the best data, have the experts on hand. Because without those building blocks in place it's really hard to take action. And that stuff is really, really hard on contracts and meetings. This is the world of trust, Guanxi, honesty and an e-mail saying go for it that changes your life. If you can act on it.

Change activist skillset continued . . .
Determination and perseverance – sometimes to an extreme.

'Genius is 1 per cent inspiration, 99 per cent perspiration.'

Thomas Alva Edison (inventor of the lightbulb,

blew up 30 laboratories by accident en route to fame!)

Change activist skillset continued . . . Determination and perseverance – sometimes to an extreme. This doesn't really need a management translation. Determination and perseverance – sometimes to an extreme is the real hallmark of activism. Social change doesn't happen overnight. (And the society called your workplace may not change overnight either.) It took Gandhi 30 years to achieve his ambition of persuading the ruling British on the subject of Indian self-determination. It took over a century to abolish slavery. It is going to take at least the first part of this millennium for us all to decide to distribute the abundance of food to people still dying of hunger. (By the way, have you clicked on www.hungersite.com yet? Check it out.)

Determination and perseverance in business is the legendary success factor. Ford went broke three times before making it. So the ability to keep going is an essential skill. And how can you develop those skills? By keeping that goal in the forefront of your mind and always expecting to get there.

Building a social change consultancy, I learned to ignore the first ten 'no thank yous' before a board wanted to hear from me. How many 'nos' can you discount to get what is right for you? The MD usually then said 'why didn't you get in touch before!'

The ability to care – emotional intelligence

Daniel Goleman (*Working with Emotional Intelligence*, Bloomsbury, 1999) added EQ (emotional intelligence) to our work vocabulary.

Here is a definition: 'Emotional intelligence refers to the capacity for recognizing our own feelings and those of others, for motivating ourselves and for managing emotions well in ourselves and in our relationships.'

Emotional intelligence is the difference between geekdom and access to the big benefits of relationship management. Java and all the object-oriented language in the world won't secure you the keys to capital unless you (a) get an agent with high EQ or else (b) develop some yourself. Soft skills hard cash.

Daniel Goleman carried out extensive research (181 roles from 121 companies) to evaluate competency models in a wide range of industries, asking, what works where? And after this evaluation of emotional competencies – defined as, for example, interpersonal skills, teamwork and co-operation, effective leadership, service orientation, he found these to be twice as important in contributing to excellence as pure skill and expertise. This held true across all categories of jobs, and in all kinds of organizations.

So companies that enable the development of emotional intelligence stand to benefit.

You are hired to perform and make your contribution to the bottom line. So what is there to learn from activists about emotional intelligence? *I am making a direct link here – saying that the ability to care overlaps with high emotional intelligence.* And although firms don't hire you explicitly to care, the business agenda now acknowledges the importance of teamwork and developing people. So the caring employee is somewhat improved in reputation from the days when the best complement you could give a guy was about his great, tough hard-nosed 'business first' attitude.

So when it comes to change leadership using the activist toolkit, the ability to care is a skill that relates to the bottom line. Spending time with the team talking about feedback from customers. Being available to discuss things offline with newer members of the team.

I believe that being emotionally effective because you care – for example, getting things done with the minimum of procrastination and drama – creates headroom to move to the next level of effectiveness – whether that's at work or a local campaign.

As the Web causes business to go for even greater integration with suppliers and customers, emotional intelligence, the ability to care and to be emotionally self-aware will become increasingly respected as the invisible glue holding the virtual process together. Teams that innovate in the real time global marketplace provided by Web technology. Global firms with software developers working round the clock linked day to day by a plan underpinned by effective leadership. Time to market depends on time to hear it.

> **So when your project team tells you that the only thing they care about is the end of phase party and bonus, be afraid. Be very afraid.**

Perhaps cultivate some new team players who have a contribution track record. Because if you want success, it seems the
ability to care needs to be right in there.

Being able to simplify complex subjects so everyone can understand and take action

Simplifying ideas for effective communication is no easy thing.
We all think because we understand something in our own
heads, it will be clear to those around us. Getting something to
happen in any kind of organization is hard. If you can't explain
the subject and get support it's impossible to make progress.

The process of explaining can feel arduous to the person
leading a change effort. Have you ever sat in a room with a
buzzy bright project leader person who is getting ever more
testy listening to your questions?

'Could you just explain again' starts to feel like 'can you just
cope with the fact I am a complete moron and don't deserve
any hope of a place on this project.'

Or have you ever been in a room where everyone is too scared
to admit they don't understand the presentation? Depending
on status and pecking order.

The new boss's first trip to the projector is usually great fun.
Smiles and break the ice humour. Then oh-my-god his charts
don't seem to make sense. Heartbeat. Quick look round to see
if the others are with you. No sign.

The reason they don't make sense is because you haven't prepped on convertible bonds or just in time logistics systems or customer relationship management models – or whatever. Well anyway, that isn't really your specialism. So you sit there. Hope someone asks a good question. Look at the clock.

OK, you could take the earlier point about the importance of emotional intelligence – the speaker should be able to read the vibes. But so often we get caught in our own showbiz moment and forget that someone out there may have been felled by the sheer power of your prose. Felled to the point of stupor!

And what happens when no one is brave enough to ask that good question and the speaker doesn't pick up on the hidden bemusement?

Well, first – what a waste. Opportunity, cost, etc. And the leader hasn't exactly got your wholesale commitment to the objective, has he? Second – immediate creation of local taboo. It will become that presentation. Third, nasty feeling about being in that room, with your best powerpoint animations, that makes everyone a little bit more nervous of their next presentation.

That is a worst case. And it costs. Compared to standing up, being clear and everyone enjoying that sense of understanding, a shared goal – it really costs. Time, budget, team spirit.

The ability to take a complex idea and break it into a simple course of action is a real skill. It takes practice. Practice like this next exercise.

Exercise

Simply my role

1. Use one slide to describe your current job.

2. Do not use bullet points.

3. Use one slogan and one image.

4. Ask two people in your building to guess your current role using your one slide (N.B. internal phone directories are not allowed).

5. Ask why (if they failed to guess correctly) and amend your spiel or slide accordingly. You should be able to get a 70 per cent correct guess rate in less than ten people.

6. Start here. With a pencil. It's OK, you can go back to the laptop soon.

   My role:

   The simple definition:

   The image most able to decribe my role:

Can you do it? Would colleagues, customers, loved ones be able to describe what you do more easily because of it? Get clear. Be able to explain.

Clarity. Pilates for your brain.

In the old days of total quality management (TQM) we were told there was only one way to eat an elephant. One spoonful at a time. There were some very odd trainers in TQM.

A determined leader or leadership team, accountable, feedback-rich

Command and control leadership has a reduced empire. Restricted now to the military, police and public institutions. Organizations concerned with growth and fast change cannot afford to risk one person leading others, who in turn lead others.

There is no activism without a catalyst. Let's take the process of leadership decision via the meeting. A group of people come together, discuss a range of items, define what might happen and then go away again without making any decision. One of the most comforting rituals of unfocused management. You get coffee, social interaction and, provided nobody takes notes or clarifies actions to be taken at the end, you get off scot-free of more responsibility. Fantastic. See you again next month. Bye.

The meeting with someone who does want something to happen is quite a different thing.

The person or persons who really want the thing to happen will want it to happen quickly and for it to really work. So they lead. In my experience of activist leadership the best examples have been leaders who do the following:

- Make sure that the effort has something important to achieve, and isn't a wild goosechase.

- Make sure that there is appropriate sponsorship: for example, in a campaign context to ensure that those who will benefit from the campaign underwrite the approach and outcomes. In a business context, making sure that a senior manager – as high up as you can get – will publicly back the project and be able to explain it's importance. With those things in place:

. . . explain the objective so everyone understands

. . . direct people to get something done, by a certain time

. . . ensure that the goal and measurement is well defined

. . . get regular feedback on better ways to do it

. . . find time for each team member

. . . give individuals a supported challenge for their development

. . . ensure some choice in the tasks

. . . respect how people need to be rewarded and recognized.

And the best leaders push the benefits again and again, talking with passion about how much better it will be when the goal is accomplished.

So in the meeting – everyone will be keen to show their contribution. Keen to show how much extra they can do. Keen to beat the deadline, make it better than the plan.

Accountability is central to the change activist leader.

Clarity on career/life objectives

Getting clear on the immediate goal is rarer than you might think. If I were to ask you what is the most important thing in your career right now, what would you say? Promotion? Being in a fast industry learning the right skills. What about life goals? Seeing the Barrier Reef corals before they bleach?

(Don't get me started. Actually look at www.coralcay.org for volunteer programmes on this.) But I digress. What is your most important goal right now? If it's finding someone gorgeous to wake up with in the morning then why are you spending zero time doing something about it? Clarity. Can you see the thing you want to achieve? You think and it becomes real. Everything you achieve in your life begins as a thought first.

What kinds of things can you do if you have this skill? Well, you'll be ahead of most of us for a start. Many of us don't dream so that we can't be disappointed. For a lot of my life I subconsciously didn't push the dream I had, because if I didn't try I couldn't fail. At school I had a fantastically stupid strategy that said if I didn't revise I could always say I could have got an A if I did revise! Excellent. I had excuses and other people had good grades, better choices.

All our objectives should be SMART. Specific, measurable, actionable, realistic and with a timescale. What gets measured gets managed.

Getting clear on your goals at this moment doesn't mean God puts your life in a concrete mould and forces you into it. It just means you have direction, which, unless you are sure you're destined to be Mr Social Flotsam or Ms Career Jetsam, is a Good Thing. Direction. Historically a combo of class disempowerment, religion and lack of cash makes many of us doubt that having a goal has any useful purpose. We had elders, betters, bosses, owners to tell us what to do. Thankfully we are in an embryonic global meritocracy and there might just be a pot of ethical profit waiting somewhere, with your name on it, if you can get your head up for a moment to consider where you really want to go. What does your ethical success look like? Close your eyes and go forward three years. Where are your current goals taking you? Become yourself in three years time from today (so the date is. . . . .). What are you doing?

Your pension is your money

I once worked for Coca-Cola. There, I've said it, so I can confidently face down any future extortionists. It was for six months (I realized belatedly for an activist this it was a very poor career move, but I was over-excited – been promised a car). While there, I met a number of people who openly acknowledged their motivation as being 'the really good pension', avoiding the hassle/excitement of a fulfilling career, calmly counting down to a good time in 17 years. Give or take a decade. Now don't get me wrong, we all need to provide for later years, and a very good idea to arrange finance for the radical fun of life in your 80s. But can I humbly suggest your pension may be a false source of confidence? The stock market has always been a rollercoaster, and the effects of stock market highs or lows are now even more wide ranging. Your change activist pensions campaign may need to get underway sooner rather than later. Action first, then benefit.

First of all, examine your pensions thinking. What are your pension expectations and what is the reality? Can you get your hands on some data? Second, how does the market impact your future? While you may never have consciously bought or sold a share, a violent shift in stock markets can still have a detrimental effect on your wealth. Many of us are 'indirect' investors in shares – our pensions and other savings schemes are locked deep within the stock markets. And we have become ever more keen on share dealing since utility privatizations led the way in the 1980s. Add a big share market boom through the 1990s, and suddenly large pension funds are all deciding to move a greater proportion of their holdings into stocks, and away from historically less safer investments such as gold and government bonds. Now it gets interesting. Your pension is firmly tracking the bucking bronco. When the market is booming (in a bull run ... remember, bull), great news – companies make lots of money from your investments sitting in those shares. Strangely, now the market has turned down (into a bear market) lots of companies have decided they'd rather not top up the deficit. So if the stock market rollercoaster stays on a downward run, this will have unpleasant consequences. The pension is your money, being invested on your behalf. If your financial managers can take the divi when times are good, why can't they cover the shortfall when times are bad? Change activist difference – don't put your head in the sand about it. Get some information.

Here are a set of questions to ask – remember that your self-esteem changes when you take action and not before. Money decisions – especially future money – is a topic on the to-do list just below lift out and clean behind cooker. Nonetheless – action makes us powerful.

Pensions activist questionnaire

Answer the following questions with:

a) yes – I know the answer here, it is

b) trying to find out – actively

c) don't know and not planning to

d) go away, I can't bear to think about it.

Questions

1. Have you got a pension?

2. What do you plan to be doing post 60?

3. What companies and industries are your pension funds invested in?

4. What fees do you pay or what does your company pay (same thing overall)?

5. What options do you have in terms of early exit (exit fees, losses, etc.)?

6. If the stock market increases by 10% over the next ten years, what will your monthly income be?

7. What other financial strategies could you have apart from pension (property, bonds, gold, keep working)?

8. What if anything is being said about final salaries schemes?

---

9. Who could advise you on your personal situation?

10. What is your plan to find out and become confident about finances this month?

Another lovely little change is the fat exit charges that investment companies have started to bill clients who would like to take their nest egg away from the rollercoaster. It is your money.

Those experts we believe are happy to share information if they've nothing to hide, right?

Perhaps this sounds too simplistic: surely everyone knows what they're doing? Wrong.

Ask more questions, practise saying no

Many millions of pounds are written off on projects with inadequately defined objectives. Caused by a variety of reasons. The change activist difference at personal level is getting very clear on the objective right up front.

For example. The boss has invited you to develop a new strategy to drive forward sales into eastern Europe. You are in his office.

'It's a big project, Sarah – vital to our European operations. I look forward to getting your document next week. Then we'll get your new team organized . . . '

'Great, I'll do that. Thank you.' Sarah tootles off, delighted to have won the opportunity to spearhead a great new challenge. Tells colleagues, gets plaudits. Drinks. Later that week, in front of the laptop, Sarah realizes that 'a new strategy to drive forward sales' could be any of a number of things. Does it mean training and developing the existing sales force to expand into new territories? Great, I'll become a glorified language broker, thinks Sarah. Or did the boss mean physically going to the new territories and building up a series of alliances – maybe even franchises? Or does it mean buying the eastern European niche competitors?

Rewind.

The boss has invited you to develop a new strategy to drive forward sales into eastern Europe. You are in his office.

'It's a big project, Sarah, vital to our European operations. I look forward to getting your document next week. Then we'll get your new team organized . . . '

'Great – thank you. Can you say a little about what the ideal outcome would be from this initiative?'

' Sure – we pick up all those little niche guys out there and bring them on board – it might mean a few noses out of joint with the sales force here – but the board has decided . . . we are buying the small competition. Can you get the document to me by Thursday. . . ?'

'Thanks – can I give you a call early next week to run through my first thoughts?' 'Yeah – fine. Bye.'

So the objective is clearer – although not crystal clear. Which is why Sarah has wisely given herself the chance to review a draft before sending something off that might not be what the board is looking for.

Projects, change programmes, merger discussions get started, with lots of enthusiasm and energy only to find (later on) that the objective isn't clear. The project – or programme – then runs on a series of assumptions that may or may not be correct. The person originally given the assignment doesn't feel it would be quite right to go back and ask for further clarification. Oh no. Much cleverer to take a tiny bit of information and magically interpret it. Remember egos are overheads! Meanwhile – the boss wonders what's going on. Didn't I ask for that report by Monday?

Don't manage by telepathy.

When taking on a change programme, the activist difference is to risk a little eye to eye discomfort to get the sponsor to clarify what s/he actually wants to happen. What gets measured gets managed, they say. And change programmes change – you may be really clear on what the boss wanted in February but now it's March and the market went south two weeks ago. Keep checking the original goal above and below the sponsor authority level. This is your career, right?

Enough on the change activist skillset for now. Seven key tools. Each with a couple of skills you might already have. And you're equipped to do anything.

Now for someone who has always seemed able and willing to take on the world and bring about change on her terms . . .

Interview – Anita Roddick, change activist

CM Carmel McConnell (interviewer)
AR Anita Roddick (interviewee)

CM *Do you feel there is a shift taking place in the business environment?*

AR A lot of great progressive thinkers are thinking about that now. How do we shape an economic agenda which is more sustainable and more humane? It's a continuous education process. I consistently have an antenna that says, give me more of these ideas to capture. Then I ask, how do I popularize it? How do I bring it down, because all I've got to offer is a phenomenally efficient distribution arena? Nearly 2000 shops, 49 countries, thousands of millions of people passing by, thousands coming in. So it makes sense that I should be able to use it. I think one of the great strengths of an activist is the notion of the Trojan horse, just being the Trojan horse is a political act.

CM *Oh yes, and doing it mindfully . . .*

AR You can't do this work in any other way. A lot of the work comes from a sense of outrage at the human condition. Maybe it's a heightened sense of empathy for the human condition. I think a lot of it comes from people who are brought up culturally as outsiders. And I was the first in this town, the first Italian. So you looked different, you smelt different, so being an outsider shaped a different agenda.

CM *What have you been doing to help people be true to themselves at The Body Shop?*

AR I think one of the things that we're tricked into is a one-dimensional definition of success. Here we understood that most Body Shop people – my constituency – were young women, under or around the age of 30, whose ethics were care. And care is an extremely powerful small word, like love. And it does lubricate the spirit, and it lubricates the senses . . . And you can give someone the chance to be part of a caring community within the confines of a workplace, which is a controlled and safe place in many ways. That means the chance to live a life that is extraordinary, or make communications great, the chance to feel that they are part of a social experiment and to feel good, to feel as if they're doing something. And we've found that in two or three ways . . .

One is we've looked at the aesthetics of a workplace, that everything should be a stamp of saying who we are, what we are. From those quotes down there to . . . you know, big funny quotes or some serious quotes there to all of the visuals around the place. The second one was protecting the notion of women and family within the workplace, so that had to be honest. So setting up a child development centre was really pivotal to helping our people feel they could be true to themselves.

And then the third one was community volunteering. So we said, half a day a month or week, go out into the community. We don't expect you to walk bloody dogs, go out and help. Whether it's literacy programmes, or working with Aids communities . . . And then I think that was a great success. The volunteer programme was so robust and everyone was being measured by it so it became institutionalized.

And this was grassroots stuff. Not just going out and giving free Body Shop samples. But the biggest challenge is taking a group of young people somewhere outside their normal environment as a group. The dynamics of good had to be kept strong in a place which was alien to them, foreign to them. Where they had to measure their greatness by how they looked after the weak and the young. This is exactly what happened in our projects in Kosovo, and in Albania, in Romania and Sarajevo, where they go on two-week sabbaticals. They'd come back and their heart was polished, you know, so it's the value of the experience. All the time that care comes from experiences.

CM *In terms of your priorities, what's in your mind to do next?*

AR I'm at the moment in my life when I'm trying to fashion the next 20 years in something that is more thoughtful. By that I mean I have accumulated knowledge which I equate with wisdom and the most important thing is sharing it. My new book is *Business as Unusual* [Thorsons].

CM *How did you create an activist mindset here?*

AR I asked myself that. So what do we do? We made it a legal document, saying that our company was dedicated to campaigning. So it became the modus operandi, the DNA of the company. And institutionalizing that sense of campaigning, and local organizing – we also spent a lot of time telling people about the myths of business. One of the myths is that community organizing and business don't need each other. We live in a global economy. So then we set about raising the profile of issues that are not seen to be the role of business. Now more people accept the role of business is shaping everything. Let's face it, corporations, unless they are checked, are criminal. They are abusing and they are wasting resources and there are no checks or balances, hence the problem in Seattle (the Anti-Globalisation Protests in 2000).

And the way that you change people with their experiences in the company is language. You do not talk the language of control, of defeat or wins. You talk the language of compassion. There's a whole new role of language that could be implemented and that really does help shape some of the thinking. Every blank space you fill, there's a place to give a message so people know.

Also you learn from experience. So you practise running campaigns. We're all activists, here; in fact the majority of people that came here were environmental activists.

CM *And you've worked this theme through, this has been your central communication message?*

AR We've only really campaigned on three areas:

1. human rights which included social justice, political and economic rights

2. environmental management and action

3. protection of animals.

So the women stuff that we did, protesting against domestic violence, that was part of human rights. And people come to The Body Shop to work if they are in gay couples because they get joint insurance, which you absolutely need. So there was a lot of openness. That's not saying it was perfect, I mean, in any way, because we were mostly manufacturing. It was very much part of a manufacturing ethos that is much more hierarchical.

But maybe my profile is high enough or strong enough to be able to take these issues as an activist and an organizer and an advocate and have the different, slightly different agenda, hence the idea of setting up the publishing companies.

CM *It just struck me that we have been talking about all the things you have done for others. Is it time to treat yourself exceptionally well and to start thinking about 'what are my needs?'*

AR You know you're very right but you know I was talking to some other activists about this. But there is a sort of psychological umbilical cord that I have with this company. About its community.

CM *Thank you for talking this through. And for telling me about your family. This activism is in your genes!*

AR Anyway, so what I can I do for you?

CM *What you have done.*

AR Really? Will that be enough for you?

Exercise

Marketing you

In corporations, there are well-known internal marketers – somehow in the right place at the right time with the right idea. Accident or design? Marketing you is part of making things happen. And so this questionnaire will help stimulate your thinking on the best way to give your light an airing outside the bushel.

Go through the following questionnaire. When you have answered each question ask the person you usually see for lunch or at break to review your answers with you.

Section 1 You are the priority

What are you passionate about? List what you feel is really important in your life. Then put a tick next to the things that you can do at work. (Yes you might have started this earlier.)

Who in the organization do you most admire? Write down why (this is often a good way of identifying a role model who may be able to offer practical help and guidance as you progress on the internal marketing of you). And please don't think only up high in the hierarchy. Think USP – your unique sales proposition.

What skills do you need to become the most valuable person in the organization. List them and assess where you are on a scale of 1–3 next to them. What does that say about your development plan?

If you have an important idea, do you make it worth the company's while to train you to do it?

Who might be your sponsor – who benefits in the hierarchy from your contribution?

Section 2 Making things change

Are there things at work that you just tolerate? What are they? Write them all down.

Do you have any idea how they could be changed, improved? Choose two or three and write your ideas as if they were instructions to be followed by someone else in charge of making some changes.

Could you get these ideas in front of your peers? Could you present to your team? Or to the school staff room? Could you get onto the agenda at the next monthly budget meeting?

Section 3 Front page you

What can you do today to find out about the route to newsworthiness where you work? Where does news get posted? The Intranet? How does the real news get made where you work?

High-profile 'actions' get issues centre stage. What would enough showbiz for your project look like? Can you imagine the press conference? The head of marketing leading a debate on your breakthrough? An article in the trade mag? A speech to the next conference of your peers? Find the stage, and be brave.

PR is a network operation. So you need to know who needs to know. How can you get your improvement idea or project, profile and performance known by all the right stakeholders? Who are they? What interests them? What can you do to reach the decision-makers with your special insight? OK, by when?

So – how was that? If you wrote stuff down, you should have a set of actions. In review with another person, figure out:

1. the things you could do pretty much straight away

2. the slightly scary but hugely exciting things

3. the dream come true scenario.

Put dates next to each thing you have decided to do.

Next, the only way to make it happen is to make it happen. When you do, keep these notes. In a few months' time when you're on that stage, you'll look back at this page. Promise.

Soundbite

Try this. Take a moment to think about your career. And now, clarify your soundbite.

Write 30 words the TV guide listing guide would use to describe a programme about you. What have been your defining moments, and what is likely to happen next, based on what has happened before? What motivates our hero/heroine? Give it a go.

Hard to get a clear summary of you? Draft it and get someone to take a look. What's the feedback?

Now we know the person, let's make the clean money. What is your USP (unique sales proposition), your special 'no one else can do it' contribution to the enterprise? To the world?

You've heard about the elevator pitch? Boss stands there. Smiles in that endearingly dysfunctional way she does because she has no idea of what you do. You have until the eighth floor to let her know you do a great job and add loads of value and she should use your talents more interestingly.

Does the elevator pitch match your TV listing? OK, refine it. Now go to the bathroom. I'm sorry? Practise being in that elevator with your boss, out loud, to your mirror. I know it feels odd, but try For goodness sake, if you can't tell your own reflection how great you are, how is it going to go in the firm? Exactly. Roseanne Barr, the US comedienne, had done years of gruelling, partially acclaimed stand-up. But the elevator pitch was the key to her success. She got her big shot at global fame from one chat show performance. People thought she was so amazing and spontaneously funny. I remember reading an interview where she later described her one minute of comedy dynamite – which she had practised, for that moment, on a syndicated chat show, for literally years before it actually happened. It worked. She knew what to say and when to say it. And got her own show. And I guess you could say she did OK re fame and fortune.

Back in the lift. Your boss's boss turns to look at herself in the mirror. This moment is really important. You could hum, look down, or look at her and smile, introduce yourself and make big things happen fast. Know thine own summary and you'll be able to let rip with a virtuoso performance at will.

Elevator Pitch – Example 1

My name is . . . . and if I told you how we could get improvement ideas from all our employees through a Web-based corporate responsibility statement, would that be of interest? Great – I'll contact your PA to set up a meeting. Thanks. Your floor? Bye. Yes nice to meet you too. (The 'I want to be an Internal Consultant Pitch'.)

Elevator Pitch Example 2

Hello, we haven't met. I work with . . . . . . on the . . . . project. I really liked what you said in the Annual Report about us being a team. On that theme, if I could show you how we can reduce our overheads, and get better environmental measures, would you be interested? Great. I'll sort out time with your PA. Your floor. Thanks – yes I look forward to it too. Bye. (The 'Lets Recycle More Because Waste Frustrates Me Pitch'.)

My First Cut Elevator Pitch. Using this format, get a 30-second introduction together, based on what you are working on right now. What are the benefits and why might you want to have some time with a senior sponsor? If you are thinking, I really don't give a flying foggy about meeting the senior team and telling them what I do I suggest you are out of sync with a) your job, b) your self-confidence and c) your firm.

Now the second stage of elevator pitch development is to add depth, drawing from your internal activist. What do you most want to do beyond the bottom line? Does the natural world move your heart? Who are your activist heroes/heroines? If you had all the time and money you needed, what would motivate your day-to-day action? How would you like to contribute to the welfare of humanity or the planet or your neighbour? What acts of charity or care could you get passionate about? Has there been a song in the past month that has stayed on your mind, made you want to fall in love and kiss someone deeply in the cool of the evening? What's happening in your heart?

When you think of how much mindshare you give the firm, perhaps you could even things up a bit – for example, try a little personal redraft time.

Now pull the TV guide, the pitch and the heart tale together. Who is this person? Get someone to help you on this. You might feel that the separate angles (or angels) are too diverse to integrate. Fact is, we have hugely divergent aspects to our being and all too often get to express only one side. Create some space to do this. It isn't easy to do in the car on the way to a meeting. Or in the dentist waiting room. Book a bit of time in the week – put 'appointment' on your electronic diary and schedule time with yourself. Bring with you paper, pen and the desire to give your own life some breathing space.

Figure out who to get feedback from. Who can you talk to? Try some people outside the sanctum and just ask them to give you some time. Yes it feels uncomfortable sometimes – but it really does develop trust.

Even if you are the fastest brain in the west, don't think this is below you. In fact the more you reckon you can do it in your sleep the more surprised you'll be by the results. Alternatively, if you don't think you're worth it, or you think things outside you need to change to make you happy, think again. You drive this.

Now this is only a bit of work to figure out something about yourself. And OK, you're busy. But listen to the signals. If you can't find time to write a TV guide list about yourself, or squeeze 30 minutes to write an elevator pitch, or simply jot down some of the sensual and loving joys of being alive – what does that say about your ability to prioritize your needs on the rollercoaster of life here and now? Trust yourself and make a little space. Ten minutes? Don't you think you deserve ten minutes when you are doing so much for everyone else?

Listen to what emerges when the spreadsheets are put away. Trust yourself to make good choices when you make the space.

This has been pretty prescriptive, I know, and who am I anyway? These are things I found useful and not too onerous. I worked with one other person to create a day of non-violent direct action involving one million people in 17 countries after spending some time reflecting. OK, I ended up in prison for non-violent civil disobedience (a civil, not criminal, prisoner by the way). But that's another story. My life now is a mixture of running the Magic Sandwich (see page 162), a child poverty charity, consulting and, of course, getting these words out. That life came directly from time on my own, productive dreaming, looking out the bus window to a better future. I can't overemphasize the merits of a good daydream (she said, returning to the keyboard after a good five minutes looking at the sky). Your future depends on what you choose to see in your mind's eye. And how much you choose to do about it.

Ask what matters in your heart.

Point that passionate purpose at the

icy walls of fear in your life

and I promise, they'll melt away

One thing that helps me when trying to figure out what is going on or who I am or what I want is this statement:

'Work like you don't need the money, love like you've never been hurt and dance like nobody's watching.'

Satchmo Paige

Active versus passive thinking

Active thinking. I define this as the state of mind of the activist. Someone determined to make things happen. Lots of people tell me that action follows thought. So if you don't feel in control then perhaps your thinking is part of the reason.

What is active thinking? Here are some examples:

- choosing a role that plays to your strengths
- believing each week is an open invitation to get things done

- being honest with yourself and getting feedback
- active empathy – finding out what is really happening with others
- sense of purpose and personal control over future events*
- feeling responsible for own career (in fact whole life destiny)
- focusing on the things that really matter
- feeling good and confident – head up and happy
- not letting anyone get away with belittling comments
- creating your own luck – taking risks
- feeling full of energy for what needs to be done
- trusting people and building close relationships
- communicating clearly and openly with confidence.

Passive thinking – the place none of us wants to be:

- agreeing to a role where you feel weak and incapable
- kidding yourself about your performance – not getting an impartial view
- viewing life from only one perspective – your own
- little sense of purpose and personal control over future events
- someone else is ultimately in charge of your career
- procrastinating – doing easy things that don't really matter

---

*For more help on helping yourself to find your true purpose, see *Soultrader, Find Purpose Find Success* (Momentum 2002).

- feeling low, lacking confidence – staying out of people's way

- allowing yourself to be insulted

- using food or drink or shopping or TV to escape how you feel deep down

- feeling like life is a pre-written script – fear of risks

- lethargic – putting off what needs to be done

- feeling a lack of trust in people – keeping peers at arm's length

- using e-mail only and hoping no one will want to speak to you today.

I'm going to speculate wildly and imagine that you want to be a success at the things that are most important to you. We all dream, we have skills, hopefully we have a sense that we can do something positive with our energies and know-how. We live in a wildly exciting time when many of the rulebooks have been discarded. You can work at home with a team in three different countries via the Internet. You can expect your employer to want some input from you on how to make things better in your job.

The old corporate standards of command and control have made way to matrix organizations, project-based enterprises where people come **You are as good as your** together with common purpose, **network says you are.** achieve the objective and disperse. Job for life has moved onto portfolio lifestyles. You are as good as your network says you are.

The activist is a mindset. Believing that you have the choice to think – to create your life – is big stuff. Choosing to focus on what is important to you and to take action to achieve your heart's desire – in a way 'to thine own self be true' – that's even bigger stuff. Those things are possible and doable and I think you're here reading this because you're ready to take action for yourself.

Creating action orientation where you work

Sometimes I think most offices are like suburbia. Frighteningly comfortable and quiet and housing the most outrageous sedition behind a very tasteful façade. Sometimes as I walk through the open-plan investment house or telecoms firm or publishing house it feels like there is a gentle Stepford stream of quiet activity going on. Those places where you see rows and rows of uninformed, mentally uniformed workers. Being uninformed is a uniform. And being uninformed encourages creative thought like metal swimsuits encourage buoyancy. Quiet offices with quiet financial returns in quiet industry backwaters. Quietly doing the continuing thing because to do something new, something creative is too scary. As Dr Susan Jeffers, in her book *Feel the Fear and Do It Anyway* (Arrow, 1996) says, creating your life is the new psychological contract – not a job for life. Fine. But I work in a very nice office and I am happy. Good – you have a foundation – for the things you really want to do.

An environment for activism requires owners and leaders who are themselves activists. Mostly. You can be a fantastic porter in the hospital and try to push improvements up from below, but usually in the meantime someone has appraised you in a soft voice in a quiet room and called you 'challenging' in a way that sounds like 'unhelpful' and you have lost a lot of confidence.

If you want to be an activist entrepreneur read *Visionary Business* by Marc Allen (New World Publishing, 1997) and remember to feel the fear and do it anyway when it comes to trusting people (for example, sharing equity, giving responsibility beyond VP Paperclips and don't hurt anyone's family life for the job).

To the dissatisfied tenants of suburban business. Time to let it go. To buy somewhere funky. And easier to maintain. Let what go? The front, the façade, the fear based on 'ignore what you want to do with your life in order to pay the bills'. Which one do you want – an excuse you can trot out (they never let me study when I were young) or coping with nerves while you take risks and learn how to make a happy, fulfilled life? You deserve to be happy and happy comes from action. Your action.

Did you think that what you do now is what you would end up doing? We have nothing to lose but our fears . . . So how can we use the tools learned so far to evaluate how much action orientation exists where you work? To also consider what might be stopping necessary development action from happening in your team.

Starting with you. Of course. Check out your own living for later score.

Do you feel confident that you personally are up for more change in your career? If so, go through the toolkit at your next team meeting and ask someone to score the team on each one, in terms of how important and how urgent that toolkit item is right now. And you can e-mail me your scores.

Change activism starts at the top

Have you noticed how the boss can have a copycat effect on the rest of the organization? Ms NiceAndOrganized has a dozen NiceAndOrganized working for her. Mrs FreeSpirit has a gang of wildchilds over in the finance department (nice dream).

Mr Open has his team talking to everyone and sharing knowledge and having a nice day. Mr WantsToGetOn has a gang of people who can't wait for the day to come to hold a coup and give him a chance to spend more time with his family. The leader extends a big shadow. Look at your own leadership team. Write the 30-word summary for the top bananas and then look around you. A correlation? Usually.

Mr Informed and his team of investigators, chasers and knowledge baiters. The people who choose to wake up and learn about what's happening with their customers, etc, suddenly end up being the people who are in charge. Being informed is the first step of activism.

And when I say change activism starts at the top, it not only means the senior team – but literally the top of you. Your head! GM foods in Great Britain were a really good thing before Friends of the Earth started pointing out a few research studies that gave us all a few concerns. Then the scientific community alerted those nice politicians who suddenly weren't sure. Then the papers picked up on that nice Peer being arrested in a field with GM crops. Now Monsanto realizes it has perhaps under-estimated the British public and is in retreat. Public trust is critical for Monsanto – without that how can it exploit its scientific investment in genetically modified food? The organic food trade has doubled since the GM adventure started. Every cloud has a silver lining . . . Now we just need to stop McDonald's buying land next to primary schools (oh yes), get those newly merged pharmaceutical companies to invest in affordable HIV/AIDs vaccines and persuade the big insurance companies to offer realistic premiums to cover inner city victims of crime. Oh yes, this is all doable and by me and you (able). Activist consumers are a fine and beautiful thing to behold. From 'Which-type' benchmarks to 'activist stand-up' Mark Thomas, we who are not prepared to take any old rubbish have power. Those nice companies didn't invest in bespoke CRM software not to get feedback, right?

Being informed is the first step to individual responsibility. Individual responsibility – quality of life is my responsibility – is the core of the activist.

Really really leading something. You'd be brilliant at it

Have you also noticed how many books there are on leadership? *Leadership and Orchestras* and *A Leader's Guide to Bicycle Maintenance* and *Leadership IP Strategy and Nutrition*. Loads to see. I guess that lots of people struggle to lead rather than manage. From Branson to Dyson, from Scardino to Fiorentino, we admire and isolate the particular genius of leaders and hope that no one will find too much leadership potential in our appraisal. Because goodness knows where that might end up. Better to put them up on pedestals and keep our heads down.

I suspect this has a link to our own frail human difficulty with individual responsibilty.

'I don't think I am a leader. I don't sleep two hours a day and read quantum physics for fun. Like they do.' As mortals we need gods, and the business leader, alongside the baccanalia of showbiz, is a more regular,

If I promote my leader onto an unreachable pedestal, perhaps that takes some pressure off me . . .

everyday kind of god for us to revere. Richard Branson understands the importance of mythology versus regular advertising spend. Ballooning his brand around the place and being action man. Guess what, he manages to refinance large swathes of the Virgin Group on incredibly good terms ... The activist difference is recognizing that we all have the ability to lead, OK not everyone in all situations – but each one of us somewhere important. We all lead in one way or another.

Trust your own leadership style to emerge in direct proportion to the chance you give it to learn.

Leadership is not just epic adventures. Leadership can be quietly introducing a new way of working that enables others to do their job with less stress. It can be thought leadership, writing to a local paper to highlight the needs of the local school. Coming up with a way to tell your new recruits about the history of your firm in a way that makes them happy to join.

This activist deconstruction of leadership is worth considering in your workplace.

Change activists don't expect anyone to lead on their behalf. No one can fully represent you and your views apart from you – so why not give it a try?

Define it, direct it and take action. Once you have tried it, and seen how much easier it is to direct and define than play politics, talk a lot and hope your ideas don't get lost or stolen.

The leadership style of many change activists is effective because it's a dispersed, feedback-rich style that encourages the leadership aspect of others. What if someone came up to you and said – you have a choice:

a) become your own current boss

b) advise your current boss.

What would you do? What would it take for you to feel you could step into the shoes and daily work of your boss? And tell me. What's stopping you from doing just that?

Is it that element of fear we all have – the words of the internal critic? Oh, I couldn't do that. He's far more confident than me, went to a better university, looks nicer in jeans, cooks a mean paella. Whatever it is, get over it!

Look at what that person actually does. Is there anything there that is really outside your knowledge or skillset? Can you somehow get that knowledge or skill?

We have managers. Managers who know budget revision spreadsheets, how to ensure the figures get to the board on time. Managers who worry about the cost of new hardware. Inspiration value minus zilch. And why? Not because they are incapable of being leaders, or are less skilled than the people who do give the orders. No. In my view we stay as managers not leaders because we follow a tide of fear and habit and the next day more fear and habit. The customers want visible improvement, not more of the same. Your staff want some direction, not a re-run team meeting. And you, gentle leader, can do it. Come on. It's your life, not a dress rehearsal.

'All the world's a stage – and we are all hopelessly under-rehearsed.'

Anon

What are you here on earth to achieve? Go for some fresh air and consider the answer to that question. Is it possible that while you're doing what you're being told to do, you deprive the rest of us of your special skills, your talent for something you were put on this earth to do? You have loads of talent. And let's face it, most days it just sits waiting inside you. All the words you never said, unwanted guests inside your head. Leading is living – leading can mean leading in small ways first of all. Then confidence grows. Work it out. And ask yourself – again. What would I attempt if I knew I couldn't fail?

This shortage of leaders not managers has implications for the way our major corporates are run. Leadership is more than being promoted at your day job. And this is something of a mystery to the directors of many companies. 'I was a hotshot finance vice-president so now I am on the board, well – I am going to be an even hotter shotter finance president.' Wrong. Being on the board is a different job from being a senior manager.

The hard bit is the intangible – governance. The steering of culture. The role model behaviour that casts a giant shadow over the rest of the organization. Deciding if social responsibility is good business is not the same as running the finance department. And there we are on another stage, still hopelessly under-rehearsed. If I really wanted to earn shedloads in the next two years I'd put a team to help corporate leaders understand ethics alongside corporate governance. Who takes responsibility for hire and fire policy in a recession? Who deals with concerns about the environment? Who makes sure that community investment is seen as strategic, alongside with financial control and new product development. The change activist difference is having corporate governance to ensure voting rights for a broader set of interests. Strong governance is the mindset behind right behaviour. What comes up on your Intranet when you search on Corporate Governance? A fast way to assess the moral muscle of your current employment choice.

Egos are overheads. Maybe you are too big and too smart to learn something new but your customers don't agree.

According to the UK Institute of Directors there is a real skill shortage in this area. Does the elevator go up to a floor where words like learning and development can't be used any more? It doesn't matter how much you earn or what your experience is. Today is another new day in the marketplace and you will need to lead change and be active. And that will constantly need skills.

I feel better now.

And what are the core things that keep the corporate body together? Shrewd finance and market know-how are important. As are clarity and persistence and all those good things. According to the milestone book on corporate governance, *Built to Last* by James Collins and Gerry Porras (Random House, 1998), there is a common story among the top-performance, long-lasting companies. The values shared by founding members. Successful firms retained values that are the senior team's core competence, but not really recognized as such. According to research shown in Built to Last, those businesses that have a strong set of values tend to stay around longer. There is proof that if your only value is making money, that ain't going to be enough to get and keep the best people. Reach for the moon and you get to the top of the trees. Aim to make something worth having and value for money and people will stay loyal even if you make some learning mistakes. Try to get a few punts out of all your extended family people for some crappy product and all you'll get is some short-term money and no future mailing list. And don't expect a warm welcome home next Friday.

A report published by the Institute of Business Ethics ('Priorities, Practice and Ethics In Small Firms', published April 2000) states that many owners of small firms are guided by strong principles even though they are rarely formalized into some kind of enforceable code of practice. The Institute recommends ten practical rules for good business conduct, shown below.

Ten practical rules for good business conduct

- Establish your core business values and stick to them or your reputation will suffer

- Welfare and motivation of your staff are critical to your success

- Remember that the owner-manager's business behaviour will be taken as the role model by staff

- If you need a partner make sure they share your vision and values

- Work at your relations with customers; they neither start nor stop when the sale is made

- Don't knock your competitors

- Stick to your agreed terms of payment

- Record all financial transactions in your books

- Find at least one way of supporting communities in which you operate

- If you are doubtful about an ethical issue in your business, take advice

Source: Institute of Business Ethics

So I am not making a liberal plea for values. They are already important to you.

And increasingly there is hunger for a life with beyond the bottom line elements. The evidence is there: values are the fuel, and contribution is an advanced service-level orientation. It's just that activists don't use quite so much jargon!

I think most of us yearn to be part of something that has some higher purpose, that sounds a bit epic and is at least half way interesting to tell our friends. Money, sex, ethics, glory (in no particular order) as some of my friends say when asked after various drinking games about their goals. The change activist difference is you persuade your ambition to come out into the world and try something. Leadership, for instance.

Can a lucrative thing . . . also be moral?

In *Built to Last* (Random House, 1998), James Collins and Gerry Porras tell readers that the most important thing about their book (a global best-seller since first published in 1994) is 'the critical importance of creating tangible mechanisms aligned to preserve the core and stimulate progress'. By the way they show how much more profitable it is to guide the organization with values that are more than profits – a simple comparison of stock exchange value proves their point comprehensively.

- The profit reflects appreciation from the market.

- The world is a very safe place for your company to play and grow.

- You make the world by the thoughts you think.

- Your business inspires friends, family and people you meet at the bus stop.

- You can mentally have an open conversation with children born 20 years from now about how you helped ensure that their world is a lovely place to live in.

- Your people share the financial rewards of the company according to their contribution, not their personal taste in shoes, skin colour, ability to run marathons or your father.

- You believe that thought diversity = multiple revenue streams = global markets.

Interview– Jane Walker, Community Change Activist

JW Jane Walker
CM Carmel McConnell

Activist tools include belief and hope.

Jane spent many years working for a major telecoms company, and more recently is involved in community-based activism. Her most recent victory was to help organize the boycott of an unacceptable land development in her home town.

CM *Jane, who are your role models when it comes to change activism, contributing to society beyond the bottom line?*

JW Residents of Hinchley Wood, Surrey (about 40 miles south of London) who successfully fought to preserve their village way of life against a drive-through car park and hamburger restaurant. The plan was to have a McDonald's take over a longstanding public house. The residents of this relatively small village decided to take action. They barricaded the pub with caravans. They gathered 5000 signatures, and went with them to present to the Prime Minister in Downing Street. They lobbied their local member of parliament – eventually leading to a wider review of the local planning law. They did traffic counts showing how a McDonald's drive-through would disrupt the village, appealed to the local council and managed to overturn the council decision to allow the proposed land development. Other communities – mine included – have fought and contributed to retaining local character in the face of generic multinational force – but Hinchley Wood won the big one.

CM *What in your view are the skills needed to be a change activist?*

JW Belief and hope – it's easy to say there's nothing we can do. That's what everyone told me in my fight against McDonald's. My view is, if you don't try, you don't have any chance of achieving what you want. We actually won.

Political skills – crucial to get the support of key people who can facilitate/help/progress what you want to achieve.

Process knowledge – know how the system or mindset you are up against works – exploit its weaknesses.

Leadership ability – to motivate people with your belief and hope.

Organization – timeliness of activities/actions. At crucial decision-making moments you need to have everything in place.

CM *How do you feel business could evolve to have greater societal contribution?*

JW Needs must – society's needs are becoming profit drivers. The sharp practices of large US companies are wearing thin in Europe. Globalization and the USA for all will fail – Europe wants its culture back! So I see business making more local adaptations or people will not buy / reject / backlash. McDonald's is experiencing this as it tries to expand into residential areas. And it is no good throwing money at charity and then treating a local community with disrespect in other areas.

Update: Hinchley Wood have won completely. McDonald's have given up and left the village. The local council in Hinchley Wood didn't exactly allow the permission for the drive-through; they didn't determine it in time and so McDonald's took them to appeal at the DETR and lost.

Magic Sandwich overview

It all started in Summer 2000 when I read an article on child poverty in the UK on the BBC website.

UK condemned over child poverty

Britain's level of child poverty surprised Unicef. Child poverty in the UK is among the worst in the developed world, according to a report by the United Nations Children's Fund, Unicef.

The UK ranks 20th out of 23 countries in the table of relative poverty – classed as families with an income less than half the national average.

Shocking stuff. Especially for those of us living professional lives with a choice of hot meals any time we want.

'School meals are the only hot meal received by one in four children in the UK.'

Child Poverty Action Group (website, August 2000)

A friend of mine who is a teacher in a school in East London told me that the staff bring in bananas to give children who ask to leave the class 'because I have a tummy ache Miss'. Quiet word later – turns out no one came home to look after him last night. When you are eight years old, what can you do? How is it possible to learn when your head is spinning and your stomach aches from a lack of food? What's the next step from not learning? Straight on to not earning. Not having fun.

Anyway. This child hunger in London is in the context of millions of pounds going through the trading screens of investment bankers, sitting less than five miles from that Hackney school. The idea that a significant percentage of London schoolchildren suffer with malnutrition does seem incredible. It is not as if we are a developing country with infrastructure problems. No. But we do have a profound design fault in terms of basic food distribution.

What can be done?

What about if we:

- get food from the retailers who can see that something needs to be done
- use trucks from logistics firms that can see something needs to be done
- obtain help with money from investment bankers who can see that something needs to be done.

I talked to my Pearson Education editor and the PR person. We came up with the name 'The Magic Sandwich Project'. I said that we could put profits from *Change Activist* towards the charity, and make sure that it linked up with other projects within existing children's charities. The Pearson people very bravely offered to go to their board for feedback and support. Before I knew it three companies had offered space, time and support. The sandwich was born.

The Magic Sandwich goals

To build a committed team of change activists to form a child poverty coalition with the following goals:

1. To work with food retailers to provide sandwiches and information on nutrition to participating schools in London free of charge. So children can learn, free from hunger.

2. To help children link their future success to eating good food now. (Question: Did Becks get where he is today on bags of crisps for breakfast? Did Britney live on chocolate bars until her first record?) We want children to want to eat better food. And we think that can be best achieved by linking good food to learning and success and earning.

3. To help businesses become learning partners to participating London schools: to potentially develop a model of local interaction between food retailers, teachers and children that measurably reduces child malnutrition.

4. To work out the best ways to support existing charity efforts in this area.

5. To attract sponsorship, funds and high-profile support, leading to more school partnerships, and even better ways of getting good food to children at school.

The Magic Sandwich action plan

Part 1 Gather information (July–October 2000)

- Talk to charities, Save the Children UK, Barnardos, NCH, Child Poverty Action Group, Children's Society.

- Meet and gain advice from teachers, children, potential corporate sponsors, education experts, nutrition experts.

- Define charity approach (best to partner existing charity, become new charity, etc.).

- Define the Sandwich Team (the steering group).

- Get charity status if most appropriate.

- Agree schools as project partners for the pilot stage.

- Form an informal sharing team with charities.

- Find helpers, perhaps from teacher training colleges, students.

- Define Press & PR.

- Find some high-energy people who want to contribute.

- Document the process and structure.

- Find office space.

- Find fundraisers to raise initial cash for pilot scheme.

Part 2 Agree approach, form Board of Trustees (by November 2000)

There are many ways we could do this. Some examples are shown below – all need to be tested.

- Local school partnering.

- One borough scheme to focus in one location.

- Use graduate trainees from corporate partners to host the foodshows in schools.

- Get support from education bosses to launch a London-wide scheme, linked to the national curriculum.

Part 3 Charity launch and pilot scheme (early May 2001)
- To make it happen successfully in a small way, capture the learning and modify.

- Media coverage to link to publication of Change Activist.

Part 4 Make it happen big time (September 2001)
- Develop final plan for expansion and make it happen with participating London schools and corporate sponsors.

- Recruit/maintain operations from small HQ and work on continual expansion.

One of my fears is that by calling it The Magic Sandwich Project we give children a slightly higher expectation of the thing. Headteacher: Children, tomorrow we will have our first delivery before school from The Magic Sandwich Project. Child: Sir, you know my sandwich sir, will it do tricks? Headteacher: Er, no. Child: Then why is it called magic sir?

A turning point was in July 2000. I spoke to a long-time friend of mine, Gill, who was leaving teaching after 15 years. She has successfully risen through the ranks to become Head of Maths. Hour on hour, patiently, kindly explaining fractions, to fractious kids. Talking to Gill about this question of how to feed hungry children. My question – how come the malnutrition figures are so high in this country with allegedly good social provision and a reasonably healthy economy? How come kids are going to school without proper food?

Sweets she said. Knowledgeably, as teachers do. They get money in the morning, eat a breakfast of sweets on the way to school, buy cakes or chips at lunchtime and then maybe eat something similar on the way home. But how can parents let kids live like that? They often don't see their parents. It's rare to find two parents involved anyway. And children learn nothing about nutrition at home and just eat sweets. It's education. I'm not sure they would eat whatever you put in front of them even if it was a delicious hot egg or bacon roll. They are used to eating sweets. Crisps are proper food as far as they are concerned. So in terms of the Magic Sandwich I really need to find out more from the kids themselves about what they would choose to do if an egg or bacon roll was to arrive in their chocolate-filled morning. Do you feel like eating an egg roll after chocolate? Don't think so. Now I want to persuade Gill to become a trustee of the Magic Sandwich Project.

How'd we do? Magic Sandwich update August 2002

In September 2001 we started delivering cinnamon raisin bagels and cereals to the five pilot schools in Hackney, East London. My Renault 5 became a bagel and cereal mobile. We delivered 700 breakfast portions a week, talked to the children to find out what they liked and disliked, changed the orders, changed the timings. We didn't get help from Tesco or Sainsbury – yet. We did get help from the Great American

Bagel Factory, who produce protein enriched bagels and sell them to us at cost – thanks, thanks and more thanks. As more people became aware of the work, media interest grew and we were featured on *London Tonight* (the early evening regional news). According to teachers the food is helping children to 'be more settled and able to learn'. It is improving timeliness – at one school we put out bagels at 9am, 15 minutes ahead of the morning bell. Breakfast clubs are proven to aid student ability to be ready and willing to learn. And when it comes to teachers, I am even more full of admiration at the sheer loving hard work, determination and optimism to help each child feel valued.

And we are going to expand. In addition to our fundraising arm, we have created a business model, a social enterprise to fund the nutrition delivery. The Magic Outcomes programme is a social leadership programme, with all profits to the partici-pating primary schools. We have a fantastic team of activists, consultants, family therapists, dramatists and teachers ready to give anyone who wants to support the schools community the MBA-level learning experience of a lifetime. And how it works is this. An organization (yours, for example) wants practical skill development, plus an understanding of customers, the changing demographics and diversity. The programme provides business skill development in a social leadership context: participants learn how to establish personal credibility with diverse stakeholders, produce a business case for change and be personally responsible for the outcome. If you can build trust with primary schoolchildren, hard-pressed teachers and parents – you can build trust with any customer anywhere. If your company or organization wants to help schools in your area, and get great leadership development, get in touch (see magicsandwich.co.uk). We have an all profits to schools programme ready to go, anytime, anyplace, anywhere.

By the way, Gill successfully left teaching, re-trained and is now an IT programmer for a small firm. And yes, she is a Magic Sandwich trustee. Thank you Gill.

04

chapter four

loyal to your firm, what about you?

how important to you is to thine own self be true?

'To thine own self be true is important because it helps one maintain purpose and dignity, aligns work with one's values, clarifies what one stands for and helps maintain self-confidence. If people were true to themselves, they would already be transforming their work, organizations, lives and the world.'

Duane Raymond, Social Activist Founder, Fairsay.com

Think it first

Do you have the copyright on your life choices? Some would say not. We get our *Truman Show* reality by virtue of the skills of ad men, right? It's all urban myth created by ad agencies and image brokers to get us to buy that jacket, those shoes. Everyone has to do whatever job they can and they're pretty lucky if they enjoy it. Even luckier if it pays well. Is that what you think? What do you think? What do you mostly think about? This is probably the most important question you'll ever answer. What do you think?

What you hold in your mind becomes the world that you live in. Those people who have got the profits, the fab careers, living the dolce vita. They thought it first. Saw it in their mind's eye. They thought it, they made it happen. So what you think about each day is your future.

Very few people actually think anything about their lives, beyond the next couple of months. Those that do have a real advantage.

Now this makes for a few shifts. First of all your leader ain't no extraordinary hero. She thought about what she wanted and made it happen. Your best friend who keeps losing his job ain't no zero. He thought about what he wanted and made it happen. OK, perhaps not always. But here's my experience. If I don't value myself, dare to think what sometimes feel like arrogant thoughts – then my internal autopilot can guide me straight into situations where I get treated with less than respect. And I say – whoops! I did it again. I was being the little servant person in my mind. No I don't mind doing that for you. Oh you want me to agree with you all the time, just because you're paying my salary. Oh OK. Fine. Small whining sound on the inside, mostly inaudible outside.

So what are you thinking about? What are you making happen?

The questions we ask and the thoughts we choose to think can make us victim or hero.

If you don't believe me, believe Dr Alan Richardson. Who? Psychologist who devised a well-known basketball visualization study. What? OK. Well-known study. For the purposes of the study, basketball players were divided into three groups:

- Group one came to the gym for 30 minutes every day for three months and practised their throws into the basket.

- Group two did no practice.

- Group three spent 30 minutes in their dorm each day, mentally imaging successful throws. Thinking about it.

After three months they were all brought back into the gym and their performance evaluated:

- Group one achieved a 24 per cent improvement.

- Group two had zero improvement.

- Group three also had 24 per cent improvement.

Implications for all of us, don't you think?

What do you want to wear today? A clear agenda and a happy face. Or don't even think about asking me out for a beer because I am really really fed up, OK? What you think leads people to buy or sell your personal brand. Why should people do business with victims?

What would you find out if you choose to investigate your own thinking habits?

Here's the first exercise. Remembering a time when you were able to get something you really wanted.

Exercise

Finding out what I want

Date _____

Place _____

Going back in time, I can remember one thing I truly wanted. (Was it a qualification, a concert ticket, a holiday, a job, a certain person?)

This is a summary of that thing, with the date of when I got it.

How did I get it? When did I decide I wanted it? What did I do?

What do I most want to happen now in my career? By when?

What will be different in my life as a result of getting it?

What do I really think about?

Enough time chewing the old pencil and wondering if it's time to get a cup of coffee. Come back to this exercise and scribble some more thoughts as they come to you. It'll be interesting.

This working out the inner workings of our minds is not something we are taught to do. Our brain is a phenomenally powerful friend and we don't even know the first thing about it. Sorry to all those out there that do.

You might get the odd moment of clarity when you decide yes, I really do know what I want. I must now have a toasted cheese on rye. And then I'll arrange a meeting with the CIO to suggest how we use my new Web content.

Most of the time we bob about, unsure of how to control the steering mechanism on our little lives.

Our lives go by doing things that some other, clearer person wants us to do. Or let's get personal. Your life. As you read these words you are in your day, wherever you are. Choosing your life moment by moment. Right now. Your external world is a mirror of the thoughts you think every day.

I found out about the link from thoughts to reality, and it profoundly changed my life. As an activist in my twenties I believed for a long time that having cash was an inherently bad thing. That I couldn't justify having personal comfort in terms of a nice place to live, or decent clothes while others lived in poverty. My duty – I thought – was to change the world and that could be done only while wearing clothes from thrift stores and jumble sales.

Then I read something about how your duty is to help the poor, not join them in their poverty. And it struck me that the time I was spending just trying to survive was time that I could be using more effectively to make changes in the world. So I changed how I thought about earning a good wage and got a great job on a community radio station and, suddenly, I was able to do loads more. And over the years I have seen that money is not inherently anything, it's just money. And it comes when I prioritize earning it. When I've been open to receiving money and have worked in ways that I know make a big contribution, I've earned a lot of money. And used that money for personal happiness and to do a lot of good in the world. I found that by thinking different thoughts about money I was able to go from being poor and angry and tired to being relatively rich and calm and only tired because I chose to work hard on something that matters. I could show you the bank accounts! And the best thing is by working from the heart and being passionate about social change and business success I've deposited both hard cash and moral dollars.

Spiritual and material enrichment.

Action

So if you spend time wanting to do something and thinking those people in HR won't let you, stop getting at yourself and take the easier option of dealing with it. Many years ago I learned the principles of Kaizen – a management approach to solving quality-related problems, based on a Japanese word meaning continuous improvement. It might be useful if you're attempting a new task – just write down as many options as you can to start. Then filter. It helps. For example. Your next vacation. Your next project assignment.

Write a summary of the questions you want to answer.

Now follow these steps:

1. What could I do?

Write as many options as you can, don't worry how realistic they are.

2. What's best?

Just keep listing ideas. Come up with loads of options. Be silly, be expansive.

3. How could I/we do it?

The greater risk might be not taking a risk right now. Are you voting stability or agility? Feeling fragile or agile? Look, you don't have to tell anyone about this list, OK? Or show anyone. So what's the most creative way to solve this? The most parent pleasing? The most entrepreneurial? The best way to please God and do it? The best way to solve the problem is probably there in your head. Isn't that good news?

4. What's the best way to do it?

Start grouping all your options, perhaps write benefits/disadvantages next to the top three. You might be getting close now to a . . .

5. Decision

OK, from that final list, what are you actually going to do? Would you still agree with this decision in front of a jury of your peers? Then great. Time for . . .

6. Action

Where, when, how, with what help? Draw the plan – boxes in a line, or a list or a load of Post-it notes on your office wall. Whatever, just go from start to finish, with a date on the last thing you'll do and a few milestones to help you see progress. Then start right now. Right now. And plan how you can . . .

7. Review

Keep checking to see you're on track. Can friends help? Can you make an honourable promise to yourself about when it will be done by and make enough time available in each week? Be good to yourself. You have taken control.

Put an end to the wishing and not doing. 'I wish I could run my own firm but I can't.' Perhaps you don't really want to. 'I keep getting headaches.' Because you tell yourself you should have a headache by now! The mind is a computer. You put in instructions and, like every literal mechanism, output is directly linked to input. Junk in, junk out. For example, if you wake up every morning and say – why am I so stupid as to still work in the department from hell – your brain will helpfully go back and list why you are so stupid. Point by point. Thanks brain. I didn't realize.

Alternatively, you can wake up and say how can I get some help on the jobs I don't understand, and maybe I'll go for a nice swim at lunchtime. Your brain will bring up a range of help for the work you've put off for two months and also get you to pack a pair of swim trunks. Which would you prefer?

A lot of successful firms were started by people who had realized this link between what we think and the world we live in. The firms that built a thought habit for every employee based on quality and customer focus did a lot better than the rip off quick for a fast buck gang, most of whom have come

Self-esteem grows from action.

and gone. Remember the basketball visualization study. Thinking about shooting those baskets for a period of time every day brought the same benefits as getting into the gym – micromovements created through imagery. But it has limits. I can't think my way into and through the NYC November marathon.

Choose your thoughts. Choose the habits of success via thought. You choose how to get to work. You might even choose what work you do. You can choose how to think about your boss or your customers or your employees. You can choose to think that the boss is stopping you doing what you want with your life; you can choose to learn from her and allow progress into your life. What do you want?

No snowflake in an avalanche ever feels responsible, I read somewhere. Thinking has a snowflake to avalanche effect. 'I can't face Terri from accounts' soon becomes 'I can't control my life,' which leads to victim status sooner or later. And it isn't anything to worry about, just notice and change it.

We can't change some of our inner make-up – I'm probably leaving it a bit late to be a child protégée – but we can decide to take action.

The existence of this much choice does rather change the view from the rollercoaster. Take your views, for example, of running a successful firm. Your profits depend on your thoughts. How much do you want? Is that net or gross? What turnover and what overheads? Now I'm not entirely negating the influence of luck and circumstance: it's just that there's no avoiding the fact that you make your own fate. And with choice comes responsibility. While we accept

Profitability depends on the ability to think the right thoughts, take action, equipped with the right network and skillset.

that someone else or some overarching lottery controls the direction of our lives we're scot-free. We don't need to take personal responsibility. I wanted to, honest, but I just wasn't allowed.

We can believe that life is just a river and we're floating downstream. Or else life is just a river that doesn't flow my way. Either way – no blame and no gain.

At organizational, divisional, team and individual level. For a lot of people – at all levels of the company – the hope still exists that 'if I work hard enough and I show up every day with the right skills and attitude – I'll get everything I hope for.' But it just isn't like that.

Career control

The ability to steer our thinking. Wow. Now imagine if your hand and your heart and your head were all committed 100 per cent in the same direction. Aligned. Complementing. In concert.

> Your hands – your skills
>
> Your heart – your emotional intelligence, e.g. values, principles, ethics
>
> Your head – your knowledge, your information

Mick Cope's *Lead Yourself* (Momentum, 2001) uses a very effective head/hand/heart model (see below) to show the powerful personal power reaction resulting from consciously combining all three aspects of you. The combination of your knowledge, your emotional intelligence (referred to as EQ, see page 100 for more), your moral force and your skills – all powering through to your chosen goal. But I can't do that! What if you could? Learning. Alignment. And a peaceful, easy feeling . . .

Head   Must evaluate project plans and work at earned value to assess the project progress against business case budget. What caused that overspend last month?

Hand   Workshop today to work through the team's progress against the plan. Will need all my influencing skills to find out from our suppliers what really caused delay.

Heart   Trust the suppliers to be open about disclosing the problems I think they've had on the project. Expect that we're all open enough to want to work things out respectfully.

People look to everything from horoscopes to personal trainers for the missing ingredient that will enhance their career prospects. Looking for guidance has been great news for booksellers (yes, I see the irony here . . .) but the message often is how to improve one fragment of your whole self. Spreadsheet skill is useful. So is being able to self coach. And lead by example.

The change activist model of career control is integrated. Your personal sense of responsibility for your thoughts, your choices. Combined with your values. Plus your ability to take action. Equals change activist production capacity.

No one out there is going to do the things you want to make your life how you want it. You can't pay someone to learn how to ride a bike for you. You can't claim that because you haven't got the mysterious rare leadership gene you're destined to a life of commerce-induced coma because the study of corporates shows that anyone can be a key protagonist in building an extraordinary business institution. Anyone. Henry Ford went bust how many times before getting lucky? Ditto with that nice Mr Dunlop and his rubber products. And Matt Groening couldn't get the BBC to take the *Simpsons* for free a few years back. Now look. *Simpsons* rules the Universe. Rightly!

A rich, happy and fulfilling life is born from changing, working out what you want and **taking action**. The consultants can't do it. Your future self can't do it. Your family can't do it. Sorry. It's you, what you think and do today that makes a difference.

Let me say that in a nicer way. Sorry for the rant.

You can create a rich, happy and fulfilling life by changing the way you think and the things you do. Your little boat and my little boat fortunately have steering and a way of powering forward. We just tend to think that it was meant to bob about and get caught up in uncontrollable tides. We forget, from day to day, that we can take it where we want it to go. Steering by personal responsibility. Powered by our values.

By the way, if anyone finds a website with all the answers, may be called allimportantanswers.com, please do drop a note to tryingtofigureitout.com, which is where many of us hang out.

Identity pitch

Picture the scene. Friend's birthday party. Food and small talk to start the evening. There is the preamble to the identity pitch.

'So what are you doing now, Andy? I see, that's interesting.'

Most people are polite and interested whatever you say. Thank goodness.

(However, being a discrimination lawyer showing interest in recent sexual harassment cases isn't good at an investment bank social event, nor being a consumer magazine writer investigating mobile phone radiation isn't good at a Picture Phone launch. Somehow the vol au vents just stay away.)

Anyway. Most of us want something impressive to say at that identity pitch moment. We want to put out the sexiest job vibe possible. And these days we tend to get a few more marks if the job contains work/life balance.

I work four days a week to juggle my ceramics with accounts work. Really? Do you ever break stuff?

We start the day with a yoga class for the team before work. We just work on stretch targets all the way!

One of the most wonderful comforters free with capitalism is that sense of identity we get from work. (See Richard Reeves' book *Happy Mondays*, Momentum, 2001.) If lucky, we can harvest valuable slogans about ourselves, which at social gatherings can be used to convey marvellous things about us. In shorthand. Yes I am educated. Yes I work hard. Yes I

The approval thing is at the core of our lives.

get up every day and go to work. So here is my identity pitch. See? Great employer, lovely lifestyle, gorgeous prospects. I really am a fine member of the human race. So like me, OK?

We are raised to get approval externally. Parents. Teachers. Peers. Then our workmates, the boss, the bank, the in-laws. If we get enough good words/strokes from the outside world then that will surely balance that little critic inside. The one that tells you not to try because it might go wrong and then what would happen. Everyone would laugh. You wouldn't be allowed back in. The critical voice has a million similar messages and we all succumb more or less to their insistence.

You know the one. Read Susan Jeffers' *Feel the Fear and Do It Anyway* (Arrow, 1996) for more on the critical message tape we all have running inside our heads. Maybe you haven't noticed it yet.

So we put ourselves through a million hoops in order to please someone outside ourselves. To get their approval so that we can feel normal. We give ourselves huge amounts of stress in order to grab some external approval – which ultimately never feels like enough anyway. And the strange thing is that the best kind of approval is internal. Now I'm not talking about becoming life's bighead – I'm simply saying that if you can develop an objective sense of yourself and, when you are doing a good job, it saves a lot of heartache trying to find the right situation in which your peers, family, board of directors say – hey Steve – great job – great guy. How much approval costs how much hassle in your life right now?

Save yourself the grief of approval seeking. Go up to that most exalted person and just say, I'm fabulous. OK! Glad you agree. (This is not a serious strategy by the way.)

The serious side is when approval takes over. Work it out. 'Well, I stayed up all Monday night doing a great presentation for the nice new finance guy and I think he liked it . . .' 'I moved from Sydney to Singapore because I didn't want to look like a troublemaker when the firm got taken over.' 'I cancelled seeing my girlfriend on Friday because some clients are over from France and I wanted to seem part of the team.' 'I wanted to get on an MBA course but they said they couldn't deal with it right now and I don't want to seem pushy.'

We've all been there. I love hearing about people who don't look for external validation so much any more. Richard Branson, CEO Virgin everything, doesn't take incoming calls during the day. So he can stay focused. He isn't bothered about trying to be there for everyone who calls. He gets to them – just before or after work. A friend of mine, Simon, cheerfully says 'job done' when the real conversation has finished. Saving years of his life that would otherwise be wasted on smalltalk. It might not massage everyone's ego but it works. And that's because Simon isn't a total approval junkie. I have to say total because he is, after all, a senior kind of corporate person and that has to include some kind of approval fixation. Right?

In this exhausting search for external validation, we often fail to consider what we would really, really, really like to do. We start a path, stay incredibly busy, get a few lines and a poor photo in the company magazine, retire to our gardens and then die.

The business world is full of people who are in one job saying that if they could, they would do something else. But they can't. Why? They don't know.

So right now right now please stop. Please read the next line and just think about it. Really think about it.

What would I most want to do with my life if I really knew I was guaranteed success?

What do you want to do? Scribble here if you want.

Today's date.

If I really knew I was guaranteed success I would do the following with my life:

1.

2.

3.

Add more . . .

Now – look at that list. In the amazing space of your imagination you have ideas. Fresh, free ideas that are uniquely
yours. There is no copyright on those thoughts. They are not
part of the psychological contract you have with your boss –
no matter how fabulous he or she is. The first step to
becoming active in your life is to think about what you would
want to do if you knew you could only meet success every
step of the way.

I know it isn't easy. I am asking you to think about things that
are of your essence. Just you. As we think we act. Simple as
that. And if there's nothing going on in your head that's
original and just about what you want to do then – well work
it out. So work colonized your brain cells and you're going to
have to develop some kind of escape route. By thinking. And
trusting. Trust yourself to have all the answers in there just
crying out for some airtime. You do.

Does your boss drive your life?

Another by-product of this search for external approval is the
career steering wheel. So many people feel their career is in
someone else's hands. Whose? The boss? The guy running the

project? Human resources? The guy who gives out the grades at high school? I really hope I get that next promotion. Let's see what happens. Quicksand, sludge, fear, no hands on the career steering wheel. It drives me crazy!!

You are in a car and it is yours and you are saying to someone else – yeah you drive. I don't mind where. I don't need to be in control.

How many times would you let someone drive you without deciding how competent they are and with no clear idea of the destination? Never! Yet we open that door each morning, climb into the corporation and let someone else steer every single day. Because the assumption is that we all have the same value set. We all want to make money and are prepared to sacrifice. Well that's rubbish. Is it because you think the boss made the firm not you? So he gets to drive every day?

Drive your own career. Say, for example, you're an IT worker. Groovy Java, html, etc. There is a migration path from IT contractor to trusted employee to project manager to programme manager to internal consultant to leader of the whole universe. Aka Big Title/Options etc. How does that migration happen? Gee, I hope they notice I did a great job on those enhancements. No. At each point there has to be an 'activist' mindset to make the next move up. At each point it is necessary to do things more effectively, to take on more responsibility. But how do you start driving your career again after so many years out of practice? Well, just go for a little journey.

In your mind.

I wonder how many of us start out saucy and end up subdued by time in the workplace. I know some lucky people start out subdued and come out saucy. Great place to work.

I suspect many of us have great ideas but don't quite put them into play. I was a PA for about a year – and it was non-stop. Non-stop service, smiles and keeping up with a volume of urgent and boring tasks. And making coffee. Despite my best intentions I couldn't get any airtime for some of my ambitions to change the office. I knew that my ideas wouldn't be listened to if I tried to talk about how to turn the team around. I was allowed to speak in meetings, but found my contribution didn't make it into the notes. I remember talking to other secretaries, we talked up a good mutiny, but that was about as far as it went. We'd more likely go out and get a chocolate bar. No Mutiny just a Bounty.

"You've been working awfully hard lately. If you need a little fresh air and sunshine, you can go to www.fresh-air-and-sunshine.com"

It was a very happy day when I got promotion to management because I felt at last my volume switch had been turned on. I'd have good ideas but no identity worth listening to. And they could have had those ideas for a PA salary! That status stuff is so expensive. How many of your admin team stand waiting to make a contribution, getting a bit bored behind a microphone with the volume switched off?

And eventually leave.

So after the big promotion, having swallowed the myth totally, I became a keen young manager with briefcase and new filofax and thank God no photos remain of the Dallas-style big hair and power shoulder suit. Well it was the early nineties. One of my first tasks was to become line manager to a group of people on a new project. These were very nice, but very quietly angry people. Why angry? Well over a period of years they had gradually been turned off the whole idea of contributing anything useful, mostly by their so-called senior managers. That familiar senior who needs to have a junior to make them feel better thing. Familiar to me from PA-dom.

A while back I read that teachers get the pupil results they believe they'll get. Bad boy gets bad boy exam marks. Even though bad boy may be bright lovely boy outside school. Pupils live up to their teacher's positive and negative expectations … and at work?

One guy, widely known as a chocolate teapot for his great usefulness in any situation, told me that they were not very motivated.

We talked. They were bright and caring and frustrated – had been looking into a pool that allowed no reflection. The hierarchy had blanked them for a long time and so they understandably saw no point in training courses, new ideas. They hadn't been listened to – for a long time.

Back to the demotivated team. We all decided to give each other a try. And over time, talks, taking a few risks in the wider organization, we three learned to trust each other. We eventually got our act together as a team and decided we would turn our project into something sexy and fun. Not an easy task because the objective was to install a standard kind of software in a large division, to time, cost and quality objectives (see I can still do the talk).

We changed from being helpdesk people to being customer champs – which felt better. We gave ourselves a groovy title and found a nicer part of the floor to hang out on. We had our meeting in a pub garden over lunch. And the project went incredibly well.

The making of our project into something more sexy and fun was informed directly by campaigning experience. On a drizzly morning in Newbury the reporter is stifling yawns as I opine passionately about the change in nuclear arms technology, 'as cruise missiles are designed to be fired first onto the people in Minsk and Moscow and St Petersburg'. And the report never got filed. So I learned to do something more interesting. Perhaps accept the invitation to speak at the peace rally with 100,000 people to speak to in a square in Gothenberg. Or suggest how to get media coverage by arranging a sit-down protest at the local newspaper in Umea (very close to the Arctic Circle. In December). I did those and, hey presto, the reports – with just the same content but a much better photo – got filed.

There is so much information flowing in and around our lives that if you do want to make things happen, you have to have impact. But there is the dread and fear of standing out and not being in favour and potentially losing our hard-won internal stock rating. We seem to chicken out, laugh it off – become powerless. The great idea, the story we have to tell becomes one we only tell our friends in the coffee shop. Not the board. Henry Ford and his distrust of what came with hands still exists. Big companies make most people scared – of standing out. Even the shiny happy people learn to adapt to fit in. Darwin works well in company life.

But you're going to be different, right?

55, out the door, still hadn't got what I went there for

We live our working lives in the hope of arriving at some familiar destination. Yes, here I am. This is what I came here for. But as our education is not so much about defining goals and plans, we may find ourselves out in the career ocean without much to steer by, or any clear idea of where we're going. And if you don't know where you're going, any road can take you there.

'Perhaps it is this spectre that most haunts working men and women: the planned obsolescence of people that is of a piece of the things they make.'

Studs Terkel

Many of us arrived in our first job courtesy of parental ambition. Or because you have to do something and why not this? As a change activist your search is going to be for the best way to live each day of your life, to stay on track for the priorities you have found for yourself. So no matter how cosy that desk gets, if you're not staying true to yourself

Have you ever done the 30-second swivel chair charge up a director's corridor with your team having placed bets on the top three?

you'll move on. Personally, I have moved on a lot and have been lucky enough to learn more about my principles from my wide number of jobs.

First of all I would like to say a fond thank you to employers who told me I was too loud. I was loud when the whole meeting did not refer to any benefit for any external customer. When I didn't do as much selling to clients as I should during social occasions. When the project manager was called 'he' and they were talking about my project. When I was told that I couldn't arrange chair races in the corridor. I suppose they had some reason with the last one, given chair casualty rates.

I found it helpful during long periods of system testing. But I digress.

I owe a heartfelt debt to earlier managers who reminded me that I really didn't fit in. It enabled me to realize that the rules were based on some people being prepared to sacrifice independent thought and deed for their future security. And others exploiting that need for security by imposing ever more grip. And that helped me be reminded to take my chances here and now rather than later. When they let go.

In those grippy firms, I believe the fresh clean air of dissent is alien. Hermetically sealed offices hold hermetically sealed management, patiently watching for their objective setting and appraisal round, leading to the next tranche of reduced-price employee shares. Meanwhile ticking off another year to the pension.

I once asked a bright and strong-minded young man why he didn't leave, given that the job and environment was an insult to his considerable intelligence. 'Because I have been here 15 years and have only another ten to go to my pension,' he said. It stayed with me like a spoken horror movie – 'I have only another ten years to go to my pension.' And then what? Travel, raise prize-winning tomatoes, buy a nice barbecue set, drink a little? Try to block out knowing you spent the best part of 25 years in that commerce-induced coma. Good grief.

Know anyone like that yourself? Help them take a long look at themselves and if you care don't let them think they've only one option for happiness – through a door marked later. The chance for happiness is here and now if we can trust ourselves. Aged 55 is not the appropriate time to start enjoying a life that usually starts around zero and goes to about 70. I will eat taste-free food until the last but one mouthful, which I will enjoy all the more knowing the sacrifice I made to get there. Not many takers on that. So why with our careers?

How many of us bank on the later door swinging open into something fabulous? The *later* door where the world is a sweet and gentle place and the car doesn't get broken into every six months. Where our bodies are healthy and lithe with more demand than supply on the romance front. The door marked *later* is simply a creation of our fear, lightly mixed with our human refusal to take individual responsibility for anything. What words do you tend to use?

'I'll see how it goes.'
'Yeah, I'll do this for a few years and then see what happens.'
'Plenty of time to figure out what I want to do.'
'I'll start studying seriously next year.'

Each one of us has a mixture of motivation for work. In the biggest and most widely regarded study of this topic, involving several hundred people in various career stages, the conclusion was that there are eight career anchor categories (for more on this read *Career Anchors* by Edgar H. Schein, Pfeiffer & Co, 1985). A career anchor is defined as 'an area of such paramount importance to a person that he or she would not give it up.' The person defines his or her self-image in terms of that priority, and it becomes an overriding issue at every stage of their career.

Now if you are like me and have spent a long time wondering how on earth to steer the light craft of our career, the concept of a career anchor seems very helpful. We each have prefer-ences. So if someone goes to work for security, fair enough. But don't expect that person to lead a risky new venture. If someone else has a huge entrepreneurial anchor, imagine day five of the new job investigating quality discrepancies in the audit team.

So for completeness, here is the full rundown. So you won't be 55 and nearly out the door before you realize what you went to work for. The eight career anchor categories are:

- **technical/functional competence** (which means being turned on by being an expert – with high talent for a particular kind of job. The celebrity chef might be one example)

- **general managerial competence** (people who really like the overall responsibility and challenge of running an organization – the business manager)

- **autonomy/independence** (people who like to run their own show at all times and not be bound by other people's rules)

- **security/stability** (designing life so as to reach predictable targets – needing to know what is going to happen and being able to plan for it. The government job, a lifetime in the Civil Service might fit this category – perhaps less so these days)

- **entrepreneurial creativity** (those who really love building new business ventures, making new products and services and enjoying economic success. Think Branson and Chambers and Schwab)

- **service/dedication to a cause** (people in the caring professions are thought to have this kind of career anchor – the doctors and social workers)

- **pure challenge** (those of us who really get a buzz from just beating the unbeatable odds at work – often in a competitive environment. For example, salespeople or athletes)

- **lifestyle** (saying that in a way career is less important than life outside work. For example, turning down promotion because family commitments came first – downshifters and portfolio workers come to mind).

So – do a quick reality check and consider if your current role, organization, profession even – will meet your innermost needs. If it does, great. If not, the quicker you can to thine own self be true the better. And if the whole thing makes you feel suddenly overwhelmed (it is quite big and grown up) try this.

Please pick up lipstick, pen, voice software mike – whatever – and answer the little quiz that follows. To check out if you plan to deal with life now – or later.

It is a *later* detector test.

Exercise

Are you living for later?

Part one. Where am I?

Here is a line.

_____

1. Please write your date of birth on the left of the line.

2. When, given all the information you have and being optimistic on top of that, do you expect to die? In what year? Write that year on the right-hand side of the line above.

3. How old are you now? Mark a place on the line above.

Sorry to be so personal.

Part two. My plans

So in those . . . . . . remaining years (work it out) I plan to (underline one of the following):

1. carry on as before. Who cares as long as the bills get paid?

2. do everything I want in my last ten years, because I'll be rich.

3. trust that I am able to handle change, so do what I most want to do now and learn from it.

4. try to bring things forward a bit because time is getting on.

5. not think about any of it because getting old is hugely gross and boring.

Part three. Personal honesty

Am I putting my life off until later? Underline one:

1. I do try to work out what I want to do sometimes, but never quite get time to do it.

2. I am going for what I want here and now.

3. It changes depending on how I feel – mostly I go for it.

4. I don't want to think about it.

5. If only I could figure out what I'm really good at . . .

This is not a scoring quiz. I just want you to write on a clean piece of paper the summary of what you came up with above. Ask yourself if you're satisfied with the rate of happiness and change and achievement in your life. If yes, great. If not, trust yourself. You can do more.

Stop the traffic

Revolution seems to be business mainstream now we've eliminated the idea of brand permanence. Adverts proclaim 'power to the people'. Buy this not that because you, consumer, can do what you want.

And recruitment adverts proclaim the need for 'out of the box' thinking. (Wonder why it's taken so long for management to be described as 'boxed in' thinking?)

A core attribute of success is the magical ability to revolutionize whatever product you need to sell, ensuring it stays in line with technology opportunities and a flash-by marketplace. Motorola fails to see picture messaging accessories in time. Loses two years and lots of market share to ex-loggers Nokia. Wal-Mart fails to see the joys of Internet grocery deliveries and suddenly car parks the size of Finland look a bit silly. Now if Wal-Mart's best people are in there thinking evolution and someone else is out there thinking revolution – who do you think wins? That's right. Stepping out with high hopes into a marketplace is no longer enough – there needs to be genuine advantage of radical thought. Your soundbite.

Your tribe. How your offering will stop the traffic. Traffic meaning the thousand pairs of eyes on your image at the airport. Traffic meaning the potential business on your site. **How are you planning to stop the traffic?**

And what about when it comes to you? Your life? Assuming you want material comforts and also a life with contribution. For argument's sake, let's say you're interested in the holy grail of money and ethics and want something to swell in the heart of your family when they think of you.

Can you borrow a leaf from the revolution in pace and spirit of business and bring an element of revolution to your own daily grind?

Right now the rules are – you have a job because you need to trade what you think and do to pay bills, enjoy recognition and be someone. Without going into a well-intentioned but dull history of capitalism, it's worth restating the fact that in order to do the big things that brought big profits, it became essential for those of us who were bosses to ensure a healthy resource supply. So – by driving up supply and driving down costs of production – it all worked out. Ford, for example, realizing that he could pay good wages, thereby creating a loyal pool of those of us who would buy the car and then need to stay in work to pay for it . . .

I'm not saying that capitalism is in itself a totally bad idea – as I eat my breakfast of food from around the world I am grateful and in some awe at the logistics sophistication necessary to get the banana from Costa Rica to North London at 35p. (This isn't going to turn into please people be nice to fruit growers and pay them fairly for their lifeblood – but do check out www.traidcraft.org for more on how they manage to get the banana here for 35p and www.hungersite.com to help those without 35p.) I am that colluding consumer and on an honest and personal level I don't imagine myself farming for my own breakfast in the near future. I don't think the people downstairs would let me use their garden anyway.

'The craft of a merchant is this: bringing a thing from where it abounds to where it is costly.'

Ralph Waldo Emerson

But going back briefly to the history – capitalism has had to ensure that the right resources are there, in plenty, to meet the market requirement for goods and services and thereby make money. During the industrial era we turned up and worked physically hard and went home exhausted. During the service era we turned up, worked physically hard, had to smile and trade pleasantries along with the product. Hard work emotionally sometimes – went home exhausted. Now in the information era we have more and more resources turning up, work less hard physically, more hard mentally and emotionally and now guess what – our soul is in the market-place. Tick the yes box when asked do you truly feel proud to work for Microsoft / AT&T / your firm.

'Activism is the rent we pay for being on this planet.'

Anita Roddick, The Body Shop

I'm simply suggesting that with so much to give as part of your job, giving to yourself is in danger of coming last.

Activists are role models if you want your life back

Why? Well – because activists are powerful. They create change. Because they represent the 'I don't agree, it's going to be this way now' that we would love to say more often. Activists are good role models because they just get on with it. How does that American vocabulary so beloved of European teens go? 'Go for it.' 'Just do it.' Shame some of those terms have become franchised by the sports corps. They sell.

Activists want to win for the world as well as themselves. Motivation and commitment are contagious. Taking action in one area means your confidence grows and your comfort level expands. So next time isn't as hard.

Taking your life seriously is another kind of falling in love. It feels good.

Taking action. And did you know that if you do the scary things first chances are the sun will come out later?

Activists in your front room

OK, today we have a team of five activists assembled in your front room, ready to take action on your life. And on this bit of paper the top ten things you need to do to get your life back. You wrote:

1. Talk to the bank about that mysterious cheque debited from your current account.

2. Get a car alarm fitted.

3. Talk to the accounts people at work about the paperwork that was meant to happen.

4. Start swimming again.

5. Phone your sister and plan a trip together.

Then there's a whole other list of stuff that you can't get to because that top five take up all your emotional energy. And every morning you run the list through in your head before you get up, so that by 7.30 it's so familiar you can't bear to go near it all day. Next morning it's Groundhog Day.

So this team of activists is going to go through your list, and help you with some underlying causes.

And because they are compassionate, but emotionally detached about your list they'll just work out priorities, match skills to tasks. They'll take your list of things to do and do them. They won't worry that they didn't get done earlier. Or have to tell a small white lie about why not. Nor watch the TV while the admin pile grows for six months. Or tell your friends about the plan again. Without action. The activists are here to do it now. OK? You'll spend the rest of the day working through that list and learning.

First of all, may I introduce Mahatma Gandhi, who is here today to help you regain your personal dignity and independence. Because he realized that without self-esteem we are nothing. His success in peacefully opposing British occupation of India was based on a clarion call to national dignity. Self-determination was the common purpose that

Gandhi envisaged. And when you believe in your own self-determination it will probably be easier to talk to the bank manager and the HR person. Over there in the white robes. I know you're surprised. Think how he feels. Sorry – cold? OK. Can we have the heating on. Thanks.

And right here we have Rosa Parks. Rosa was a seamstress by profession. Also history maker and catalyst of the American civil rights movement. You don't remember the story? OK. It was December 1955 in Montgomery, Alabama. City buses at that time were segregated, with only white people allowed to sit at the front. Nice. Rosa was asked by the driver to move to the back of the bus. She refused, was arrested, and her arrest sparked a boycott of the segregated bus system in Montgomery. She risked everything to make the point that African American people would not take being treated by whites as second-class citizens. Living in the same town, and among those offering the Rosa-inspired boycott their support, was a young preacher called Martin Luther King. Rosa's act brought the media to Montgomery and led to ten years of marches, speeches, and a wide range of equality activism, before the segration laws were finally ended. Rosa is here to help you work out what is most important to you in your life. She is going to sit here with you for an hour or so and talk about what you won't tolerate in your life. And what you want to make happen. Do you like the way your job makes you feel? Do you have a level of contribution you would like to make in the world? Only later when it feels less scary. Rosa might have some insight. And yes it would be nice if you could make some tea for Rosa while we're talking.

Sitting next to Rosa is Anita Roddick who has a bit of advice on how you, as one ordinary person, can win against big financial institutions. I know your action list says only talk to the bank manager about a cheque that you don't think should have left your current account. But let's face it, right now that cheque is the difference between being in debt and going out for pizza tomorrow night. Anita is going to talk through a few financial strategies to help you realize how you might make more of the skills you've got. And find out if you have some fantastic way to make money that you perhaps haven't quite worked out. Because she founded a business from her front room, on her own. Which is now worth about £250 million pounds. Check that. Also, Anita will be quite good to talk to about dealing with the clients that you want to do business with, because Anita took on the might of Royal Dutch Shell to support the Ogoni people in Nigeria and by her actions offered a huge level of support, leading to international fury at the involvement of Shell and harrassment of Ogoni activists opposed to Nigerian government corruption. So she'll have some useful insight into turning things around with that bank manager. And, yes, you can show her all the things you bought from The Body Shop to prove how good you are.

Over here we have Lao Tse, from China, who is credited with being the original writer of much Taoist thinking. Lao Tse is going to help with your procrastination. As he wrote, over 2000 years ago, 'a tree as big around as you can reach starts with a small seed; a thousand-mile journey starts with one small step.' You might have heard that before.

Now I want you to sit down while I introduce the final member of the activist team. You might get a bit of a fright. I know you're a bit shaky from meeting heroes from activist history already.

Do you recognize this young person? Yourself aged 13? Before you forgot those dreams about playing for Manchester United. Yep. The person who wrote to the local paper to plead for compassion for battery hens. Who argued that kids should be in the government because how could grown-ups possibly understand what was needed in schools. Who dyed his hair black and white and got banned from school for two weeks. This is you, raw, uncool and very, very feisty. And apparently wanting a toasted cheese sandwich. Anyone else for a cheese sandwich?

With the help of these four activists, we'll have that list over in no time at all. Activists will help you get your life back. Point the right people at the thing and it gets done. And my experience is that each one of us has some of Gandhi's coalition building-skill, some of Rosa's bravery, some of Anita's ethics and commercial determination, some of Lao Tse's instinct for peace and the greater meaning of it all. And surely we all retain some of our young passion.

Life might dilute your dreams but they still hold. Trust yourself – trust that these skills exist. Trust that the compassion gene stays fit and strong even though your high hopes might get a little worn away. Your life is your own to steer and if you feel it is slipping away sometimes, that's OK. As long as you really know what is important and where you plan to go, a bit of delay is fine. The tragic option is allowing your whole life to move by without once asking what you have been put here to contribute. And feeling overwhelmed for years when a change in the way you think and accepting a bit of help could have turned the whole thing around. As I once read.

Life is like an automobile. It gets driven from the inside out not the other way round.

One final thing about working activist magic in your own life.

Imagine you could call together the activists you most admire and get their advice on the things you most want to do. Don't have to be famous people. People you have met with impact, heart. Good communicators. Who do you admire, someone who gets on with it? And makes a difference in the world. Your parents might be a good start. Mine are great, although unfortunately both dead. Which means that I wish I'd asked for more advice earlier on.

Another tip for free.

Exercise

Who is on your personal list of role model activists?

Some will be more famous than others. They are people who inspire you to a higher level of hope about what can be achieved.

Who do I admire?	Why are they an activist role model?	And what can I learn from them
1.		
2.		
3.		
4.		
5.		

And there's always the toolkit checklist.

Clarity of objective – usually a single focus
The most important thing for me to achieve in my life is:

Absolute determination to win
I know I will have succeeded when:

The ability to care – emotional intelligence
Getting there will mean developing allies. Who is on my team?

Being able to simplify complex subjects so everyone can understand and take action
How would I summarize my goal, how I am going to get there, and what do I plan to contribute?

A determined leader or leadership team, accountable, feedback-rich
What are my leadership skills? What is my style?

The ability to make decisions quickly and act quickly
What has to be decided this week? What can I actually do today?

Non-hierarchical approach to contribution – everyone can make a difference
Am I allowing everyone to have their say?

Being motivational communicators
Have I got my elevator pitch honed? And a press release?

Physical stamina
Activists have to be able to take action. Do I have a plan for being well?

Sense of self in the world – I know who I am and what I can do
And I'm unstoppable!

Righteous anger

If you want your life back . . . *get angry*.

This book assumes you have to work and that you are not always 100 per cent happy with the control you feel you have over your future. OK? Then let's talk about a workplace taboo. Let's talk about anger. Red raging fires blazing this matters to me anger.

As a non-violent organizer for social change, my life has included times when I have been really angry. So angry that

I had to do something. There is a point where dissatisfaction with what is, causes a person to create what is not. There is a last time your boss starts doing e-mail when you're talking to her. A last time you read about the closure of a vital local service because it doesn't make enough money. A last time you see the heroes of industry evade every single question about how many redundancies result from the merger. The last time you read about a person who died aged 32. At work.

Passive = virtuous, active = dangerous.

You have the right to anger. You have the right to voice your anger. The salary doesn't melt away your emotional core – you are expected to push the adrenaline up when the project needs you to. Maybe you thought anger was not part of the psychological trade.

Angry is not the same as violent. Violence does not work. Fighting for change just causes more fighting, not more change. Violence isn't far from egotism. Allowing the self to lose control. But anger – that is part of the process of change activism. Absolutely.

Angry activists today besieged the Big Oil Company Annual Meeting to protest involvement in developing world politics.

Angry manager ... (insert your name) today held frank open meeting with boss to insist on respect for different ways of working.

One of those doesn't ring so true does it? Do you have to be sacked before you stand up for yourself? Do you have to become an activist? Do it now before you forget how too. You did already? OK.

Activism is a high. It draws on our human capacity for fight or flight. Change often results from the adrenaline of anger, a controlled sense of outrage at the wrongs as well as technique and perseverance. If you want to get active to change things, start with the things that make you – and others – rage with reason.

For example – the campaign to restore potted plants on every desk is likely to make no odds to anyone – apart, maybe, from the local garden centre. (I know this will annoy the many plant lovers – don't take it personally.) The *Potted Plants Now Newsletter* may not make its way into the briefcases of the masses. The Potted Plants Now meeting in the pub at 5.00 pm this Thursday may be sparsely attended.

If you found out that the board is buying a new subsidiary and planning to pay your opposite number twice your pay – despite the fact of monthly profits and a legal requirement – would that make you angry? If you found out that the pension scheme where you work is mostly in the arms and tobacco trade (and therefore losing money) would that make you angry? If you found out the new guy is on half – or double – your salary, would you be angry? What if your employer is harvesting your skills because he thinks you won't mind not doing anything new because you are 'after all doing rather well bonus-wise'?

At some point – you get angry. When you are angry, you are sharper, more urgent and everything is in close range. Getting angry on behalf of your own interest in life is a good idea. Getting angry so that your heart articulates your needs and doesn't say yes sir and then go home feeling murderous and hurt. Getting angry so that you remember that you are alive and have as much right to happiness as the next creature. Getting angry so that the things that are screamingly painfully wrong get some heat on them. Not just a polite TV interview, or a letter to the CEO. Anger makes others accountable. Anger means action. It is not the easiest place to be in but, gentle reader, if you are not angry (some of the time) you ain't living.

Now anger within the workforce is clearly something that might take extra resources to handle. Anger might be unpredictable, volatile, might challenge the day-to-day sweet flow of supply channel revenue into the trouser pockets of shareholders. So let's not let the workforce get angry. Let's do all we can to dissuade our people of their emotions. Traditionally you lost your job if you lost your temper. Now tempers in the right context may be admissible. OK, not where I worked. Especially as a woman who might just go hysterical if someone dared call me hysterical!

Being angry sometimes keeps your organization healthy. Assuming you're a grown-up and you want to do something to improve the way your company provides products and services. The organizations that don't allow you to vent your spleen when someone/something screws up may be missing a big fat trick.

What is the greater danger? That things are out in the open and people speak their minds when something goes wrong? Or that the firm can feel safe at night knowing it's employees are asleep emotionally during the day?

Anger as an emotional state sometimes is very real and very hard. You may cry with anger, shake with anger, say unkind things with anger. But if you live in a no-bad-feelings place called where I work then chances are you're also inhabiting a no-good-feelings place as well.

Finally – I am delighted if you are not angry. If your career track is clear and you are ascending and learning loads and having fun. Long may it continue.

Becoming de-institutionalized

My younger sister Carolyn lives and works with people who have a range of special needs. Some of her friends have spent time in mental institutions or prison. Some in both.

She told me about one person who had to become de-institutionalized – see if it reminds you of anything.

May (not her real name) had been in a mental hospital since her late teens when she had had a baby without the permission of her family. They decided she was insane (it was the late 1950s) and had the baby given up for adoption. May was so distressed by the forced removal of her baby that her family decided to section her. (Section means to get someone committed to hospital – at that time they needed a medical practitioner and a policeman to make that decision, and it could happen – as it did with May – on the say-so of her family.)

In the late 1980s May's daughter found her. And after a long and harrowing time, May gained her freedom from the mental institution in North London. Carolyn lived in the same house – and watched her transition from person on major tranquillizers to relatively stable and happy person. With her daughter's help.

- May didn't know how to deal with money.

- She showed a childlike pleasure in being given a gift or compliment.

- She found it hard to form her own opinion, e.g. what TV programme to watch.

- She lacked confidence outside subjects she knew well – like knitting.

- Whatever the doctor said was always right.

- Same with anyone in authority – solicitors or bank clerks terrified her.

- She had trouble getting used to freedom, e.g. going outside when she wanted to.

- She kept to routines, which meant she felt safe – the same food same time each day.

- She didn't feel able to speak up for herself – her voice had grown incredibly soft and quiet through years of just saying please and thank you.

- She didn't know how to relax – she had to be doing something – usually knitting.

- Going to the shops was a real treat – having a chance to choose what to buy for herself.

- She was scared if someone raised their voice nearby.

I got to know May a little from socials and in the house. Apart from the tragedy of her life I was struck by the similarities of someone liberated from a mental institution and how I felt when I left big corporate life after only five years. Yes, I know that it is a completely different thing – I do. It is not really comparable. But please hear me when I tell you of the feelings of powerlessness, of wanting someone to be in charge and tell me what to think – May's life had some resonance for me. We all deserve to be free.

Work/life balance

'You put your whole self in – and your whole self out

In out in out

Shake it all about

You do the hokey cokey and you turn around

That's what it's all about'

We need to create balance in our own personal lives in order to create balance on our planet.

Devon, southwest England, in May. The hedgerows are dotted with tiny pink flowers, bluebells spring out, buttercups add a vibrant yellow. The air is full of birdsong – blackbirds are nesting and very happy about the whole thing. White seabirds share newly turned fields with crows. Rivers host the brilliance of turquoise kingfishers and yellow-headed finches. There is a gentle warmth in the air, the soil is rich and fragrant – an almost tropical green abundance. There is a National Trust coastal path that will take you along clifftops overlooking pale aqua sea, sheep grazing easily with their lambs. Towns are infrequent and ancient and almost all have the same mellow way.

And guess what – the place is almost empty during the week.

Weekends – cars, families, kids and the woodland walks are full of happy hikers. But not during the week. No. Sorry, not for you old buddy – nature and her astonishing gifts are only available to the salaryseekers after 7.00 in the evening (is it worth putting the kids in the car for an hour, dear – I thought not) or at the weekend.

Another outdated pre-personal power concept that we haven't revised.

By becoming passionate, focused and more effective the world opens up into a place with more open doors to nature. How? More of the above equals more marketable, which means terms get negotiated.

For example, BT now says it doesn't matter where its knowledge team works, or what hours it keeps or how it dresses. As long as it signs up to the project and does the thing that needs doing. So right skills, right employer project management means no dress code. Devon during the week. Seeing the kids before they become teenagers. A four-day working week. Getting out of the office at the end of a good eight hours rather than waiting until your rival for promotion goes home.

Stress – your choice

Stress is inside out not outside in, according to the psychologists. Just like the car. Just like your career. Oh dear. Back to taking personal responsibility again. Just when I thought it was finally safe to blame capitalism and my parents for something!

Stress indicators

Work/life balance is not something that happens to someone else. Active not passive thinking means we make the decisions for ourselves and expect that our decisions will have real impact. The boss is doing the same thing!

Ambiguity
Is your role clearly defined? What can you do to ensure there is a more practical definition so you are not trying to please too many stakeholders?

Workplace environment
Air quality, light, ionisers, access to water ... they all contribute to your well-being. Action needed?

Your inner critic
I once had a friend who stayed at work every day until 8.00 in the evening because he wanted to clear all his e-mails on the day they arrived. Like, hello! Half of them were non-urgent copy in junk and he still sat there, opening deleting, opening deleting, while a perfectly lovely evening with his loved ones slipped away. Do you overdo it because of perfectionism? Do you spread yourself too thin trying to please everyone? Ask

yourself – what would the voice in your head say if you left every evening at 5.30, or eight hours after you came in? Write that dialogue down and work on it. It's just a critical voice, not reality!

Timescale stress

Do you have times when the workload doubles or the project gets particularly hot? Is it your organization's culture to firefight every regular activity? Try some planning. Here's a quick idea.

Differentiate between tasks which are important – i.e. must be done – and urgent – e.g. must be done now. The high importance, high urgency tasks come first. If you're anything like me (do things you fancy doing first, e.g. social e-mails!) the simple discipline of tackling high importance, high urgency tasks first will really improve your day. And feelings of virtue spill over into everything else you have to do.

'I don't know the key to success, but the key to failure is trying to please everybody.'

Bill Cosby, US comic and social entrepreneur

Exercise

Choosing a low-stress career

A few questions to help you figure this one out.

- What would my ideal week include?

- What do I personally do that contributes to increased workplace stress?

- What would I like to do that I can't do right now because there's no time?

- What would it feel like to have all the time I needed?

- What are the things that happen again and again – that I might be able to plan for more effectively?

Go through this and imagine that you are going to present 'my first low-stress week' to your best friend. Use your diary or memory to work out what usually happens. Include work events. Indicate 'high, medium or low-stress potential'. What is the plan to deal with high-stress potential events? Who can help?

Here is the outline:

My first low-stress week

Worksheet for week 1

Starting . . . .

Finishing . . . .

Day planners

Day 1

Regular events . . . .

Potential add-on events . . . .

Potential stress events . . . .

How I can plan ahead . . . .

Who can help me . . . .

What can I do next time . . . .

What have I learned . . . .

Day 2

Day 3

Day 4

Day 5

Day 6

Day 7

Remember that working a short but awful week is more stressful than working longer hours, enjoying every bit of it.

At the end of week one review and evaluate the events that have caused you to stress out. Do they form a regular category?

Now what action can you take to improve this? Don't expect overnight salvation – identification leads to awareness, which leads to action. Slowly. Give yourself a break. Activism is a virtuous circle – the more you use the tools the more malleable the ether of work becomes.

Dorothy Parker, I believe, said: 'no one can make you feel inferior without your permission.'

No one can make you feel inferior without your permission.

By changing your mindset and using the simple activist tools you will become more able to plan and do to thine own self be true.

Don't worry. Scared and lazy is normal

'I see the better things, and approve. I follow the worse.'

Ovid (43 BC–AD 17), Metamorphosis

'I used to have a handle on life. Then it broke.'

Bumper sticker, M4 motorway, England

Commerce-induced coma can be very comfortable. Many of my months of stupor were very pleasant. Occasionally I would break out and dream. Of working in a team where we could all have exactly the same conversations, with or without the senior boss standing there. Then I'd go back to wondering about who would be at the next steering group meeting, or spreadsheet formatting.

The long days of volume without inspiration did have a gently numbing effect. I still feel it. My PhD in procrastination was honed to perfection during those days.

When a rocket leaves the earth, it uses up almost half its fuel load in the first 20 seconds breaking free of earth's gravity. Getting up and away from commerce-induced coma is just the same. Your values and where you have got to get to are fuel. And the first five minutes of change is definitely the hardest.

In 1961 Kennedy got the US population behind the dream of a man on the moon by the end of the decade. This became urgent – foolishly, perhaps, given our other earthly difficulties – but it was a compelling vision, there was a crazy heroism about it. And it happened. Did you see the millennium celebration programme, showing the most popular moments in TV history from the last 1000 years? Guess what was number one – yup, Neil Armstrong's 'one small step for man, one giant leap for mankind'. In the UK, that was voted number one out of everything else we've watched.

Talking to friends about that we realize that we have, at times, had our own equiv- alent space race happening, when we knew – if only for a second – the thing we most wanted to do with our lives and what would make our

Going after the thing that makes you feel most true to yourself is your birthright. Your destiny perhaps. Your space race.

talents and aspirations burst into life. Those times are precious and, for most people, surprisingly rare.

Dreams are the magnets for thine own self be true. Being true to yourself takes courage and the normal activist doesn't always feel brave. However, being scared to do what you want and living a same old, same old life – is much more frightening. The deal is – unless you really do what you want, the bills only just get paid anyway. Because you make more with passion . . . Do what you want through work – yes, and power. Happiness. And to contribute.

But it's going to take almost half your fuel to make just a small move out of your day-to-day gravity.

Moral choices

'Money is my only goal, I've never thought about giving a damn'

So how do you stay radical? Is it even desirable? At university we all knew people who had been so fresh and funky and who are now in need of a serious 'check-up from the neck up' to see if there is anyone still there. What happens?

Maybe we just tell a good story about not caring about our lives anymore.

I grew up. I got older. I realized that you can't change the world. I realized that you can't have things all your way. I realised it wasn't going to pay the bills and we have kids. I realized it was too much like hard work. I realized that I wanted an easy life, realized I was too scared to give it a go. Of course I still care but I don't watch much news now.

Somewhere along the line I realized that a small number of my colleagues were just not interested in the well-being of their peers, or the gap between rich and poor, or the growing environmental threat. Simply not interested. And not likely to change. The things that they cared about were likely to be family, kids and their career. That showed a loving streak – but it often ended there. For many of us, the raison d'être is to study, to get qualifications, to then have to earn our way to a better standard of living. Those concerns take all our energy. We quite naturally give our focus and energy to whatever it takes to get the promotion, the raise, and the external approval. Then, at some point, we progress to the promised land. The house looks great. The car gleams and screams success to the neighbours. The vacations grow more exotic. For many people that is the happy ending. Life without financial worry. For at least an equal number there is evidence that the dolce vita could be sweeter. There is some isolation – a sense as you get older that work skills are your only skills – so what happens when the firm no longer wants you. The money goal doesn't seem to be as much the answer you first hoped.

'I do give a damn, and I show it'

Another small category of colleagues really made sure that their lives included a daily refresher in the values they held dear. Their care about the environment would mean a quiet campaign to ensure paper got recycled. They would be the ones raising money for a local shelter. Taking a stressed colleague out for a chat. Their values were in clear evidence – and perhaps they ran a risk of being seen as do-gooders – lacking the ruthlessness that corporations used to cherish.

'I used to give a damn – in fact I still do – but right now I'm too stressed, knackered, overwhelmed'

The next category I have encountered includes colleagues, who speak of values that extend beyond their immediate circle, who have not found a way to further their career and do the right thing by their value set. They had often lost sight of what is most important in the day-to-day struggle to keep earning.

This seemed to me to be the biggest group. The pull of immediate tasks, of working and eating and sleeping and somewhere the lovelife, the family, the laundry. So much to do in each week and every week the list of things to do from last week gets longer. Until some things get lost. Below is a grid exploring values, evidence and ideas for a potential action plan to ensure that values are being lived here and now and not in some mythical time after work and before we socialize.

My values now matrix

'What is important to me	Evidence	Plan to integrate my values	Discussed with
Family	I need to see my parents regularly	Work out a regular time now rather than just drift	
	Talk to my sister and keep up with the kids	Tell my sister about this!	
Recognition – financial	I want to earn £40 000 by 2001 Buying a new double bed	Project team gets PM (Project Management) skills and targets	Marketing team
Music	Having time to see live music	Go to FABRIC (a club)	Agree with Mark to go to concert
Freedom	Being able to go on holiday when I want to	Actually do something next week	
Honesty	Feeling people say things to me not behind my back	Don't just go along with office gossip	

'I am only one, but I am still one. I cannot do everything but still I am one. I cannot do everything but still I can do something. I will not refuse to do something I can do.'

Helen Keller

Staying on course

In her great book *Feel the Fear and Do It Anyway* (Arrow, 1996), Dr Susan Jeffers gives an example that has given me great hope in my off-the-beaten-track career. Apparently (and I haven't checked this with any pilot types) for 95 per cent of the journey, a plane travelling

Let's face it, everyone has times when virtually everything feels too scary.

between London and New York is off the plotted course. Compared to the correct flight path, the plane is constantly deviating slightly north or south from the exact route. Fortunately, pilots are able to assess exactly how far off course, using the instruments, and make the necessary corrections. The plane lands safely, successfully in New York having been on the right path for only 5 per cent of the whole journey.

So big deal if we can't get on with the things we should be doing this morning.

As long as we know where our own personal New York is, our goal, our destination. And – and we know the values we're being guided by, we will get there.

It's a valuable investment to spend time figuring out where you want to get to. And what is important to you. Because then you have your destination and route map. And the plane is your values. How you get there is motivation and that is provided by doing the things that you believe are priorities.

With that information, I promise you, the naughty morning spent watching *Tom and Jerry* and *Star Trek* re-runs with a large bowl of popcorn won't be such a bad thing. 'I turned off the TV and, looking at the cockpit instrumentation in my heart, realized that if I was going to get promotion it probably would be worth making a slight adjustment to the planned day. Perhaps, instead of a bit of retail therapy in the mall, I might just do the research for that report I've been putting off. I made the change, did the research and successfully landed up in the marketing department the next month . . .'

I know it isn't all that easy. We don't have the space to work out our destination and construct the plane. We have, after all, got laundry. And a long day with the in-tray from hell. This commerce-induced coma thing that causes a lot of us to wake up several years after taking what sounded like a perfectly challenging job. Only to find we got promoted in nothing but somnambulism.

05

activism and peaceful dissent

I AM NOT a natural explorer. If I find a new place to live I tend to believe that the rooms should remain more or less intact with maybe a few cosmetic improvements. My partner Catherine doesn't have the same view. Her idea is to make the home as close to her ideal as possible. So if the bathroom is where the dining room should be in her view . . . she changes it. Taking walls down, plumbing and electrics and the whole thing. I feel pretty excited about putting up a new coat of paint. Catherine wonders how to create a roof terrace. (And by the way as an employment lawyer she has had the same impact and success.)

We just have different boundaries.

Perhaps the shaping of history has some similarities. Many of us cruise into the reality we are born into, believing the walls of our lives are a permanent feature. 'You were born into a distinguished family of marine cargo insurance brokers, so no prizes for guessing what's waiting for you, my boy, after the old trip to Uni.' Son dressed as and listening to Eminem smiles ironically back. Sure dad.

The rules are there to be obeyed and there are a limited number of options for change. But for some reason, there are people who look at their societal and cultural home and ask – what needs to change about this, for me to live here?

CNN beams into 15 million homes. Twenty million business travellers take off per year (the majority in planes).

We have seen the rise of the new digital citizen, brand wearing, business oriented, wired and inspired to greater things. But we also have how many new wars going on around the world? We live in a world where the threat is death by obesity or starvation – depending on where your parents happen to live.

Time to hold hands up – we haven't really prioritized fair distribution. We haven't yet decided to divide out our globally abundant supplies of water or food, so that health can begin to be regarded as a birthright. I want my nieces and nephews never to be hungry. They are unlikely to be – thank goodness. But in London we have a situation where up to 1 in 15 kids suffers from World Health Organization standard malnutrition. Where according to the Mayors Report 50 per cent of school children live in income poverty. The UK is the fourth largest economy in the world. Billions of dollars of financial transactions flood past our City trading screens each year.

Humanity doesn't seem to have prioritized the basic welfare of every child born quite as much as the accumulation of money for the minority. So there is still plenty of challenge when it comes to creating a more beautiful and comfortable place for us humans to live – on this planet. *The Cluetrain Manifesto* (ft.com, 2000) says: 'We long to be part of a world that makes sense rather than accept the accidental alienation imposed by market forces too large to grasp, to even contemplate. And this longing is not mere wistful nostalgia, not just some unreconstructed adolescent dream. It is living evidence of heart, what makes us most human. But companies don't like us human, they leverage our longing for their own ends.'

We are caught in the glare of brands and imagined stares of those we look to for approval – our families, our careers, our earning, our status. Does my bum look big in this?

Plus we give our all every day to whatever the bosses want us to. And therefore I'm too tired to be inspired. Who do you know that has any thinking time left, never mind extra free time to use on things like ending global poverty? Who do you know that manages to really get time to chill at weekends any more?

Change activists – the quest people, bringers of the new views, don't tend to get good press. The better way sometimes seems like more hard work to the over stressed.

In this century people such as Gandhi and Rosa Parks and Emily Pankhurst and A. John Bird (who started the *Big Issue* magazine to help homeless people) have had the courage to express their discomfort with the way their society was ordered. Through enormous personal will and shining example, caused others to see the benefits of a new situation. They have not all demanded riots. Nor have they allowed those who want to riot to sit easily in their company (which I think has lessons for the planners of US and UK anti-capitalist protests around the world).

These people caused a huge shift in the mindset of their contemporaries and were able to insist through reason and popular debate that theirs was a better way. Gandhi believed the people of India had the right to self-determination, and that this could be achieved without violence. This was a fundamentally outrageous assertion. The British Raj had been in place for 150 years, ruled with effectiveness and, for the most part, benevolence. Among the Raj in the 1920s – when Gandhi began his widespread campaign – there was a sense that 'the sun would never set on the British Empire'. The status quo was more embedded than our modern global US flavour business environment. And yet Gandhi mobilized over 500 million people. How? By articulating the future, by developing and then expecting a sense of self-esteem to flourish beyond the reach of colonialism, among ordinary Indians. He made it happen by personal example. He made the unthinkable speakable and then the impossible became real. Just as I expect us to eradicate poverty on this planet in my lifetime. We eradicated slavery in the last century. We are making progress. We are not fast or cohesive. But as a race, my hope is that we'll start to trust our good instincts and realize our power.

History doesn't necessarily change when we all decide to do something different. History is made to change by those who decide to *do something different and then take action*. Some people are here to move humanity one step forward. Those people were born and raised with the same kinds of expectation as you or me. They were brave and passionate souls – but also human and fallible and prone to times of being scared and lazy. No one said Gandhi wasn't terrified. He was – but that didn't stop him from changing the face of history. Peacefully and with dignity.

Campaigns and lessons for change

Here is where the link between effective social activist and empowered worker comes in. Both have to make change happen. Looking at some high-profile campaigns there are certainly generic lessons that apply to any change programme anywhere.

From: Chancellor DebtG7Summit
<Chancellor.DebtG7Summit@hm-treasury.gsi.gov.uk
Reply-To: Chancellor.DebtG7Summit@hm-treasury.gsi.gov.uk
To: carmelmcconnell@hotmail.com
Subject: DROP THE DEBT NOW
Date: Fri, 14 Jul 2000

Thank you for your e-mail supporting the campaign for debt relief.

The UK Government will use the opportunity of both the G7 Finance Ministers' meeting next month and the G8 Heads of Government Summit in Okinawa to discuss the issue of debt relief. At both of these meetings we will be reviewing and encouraging progress on the HIPC initiative, as well as discussing the part that debt relief can play in the wider issue of development.

Gordon Brown

Jubilee 2000 Campaign to end Third World debt

The objective The wealth of the three richest people in the world exceeds the combined GDP of the 48 poorest countries.

Every man, woman and child in Sub-Saharan Africa owes £240. The total debt owed by developing countries to the west is $350 billion. The objective is to work with finance ministers and world bankers to effectively cancel that debt.

The team Ian Marks has founded the Network for Social Change in the USA. The campaign, headed in the UK by Ann Pettifor, is the biggest international campaign since anti-apartheid.

The values Public education, gaining public support. In an interview Ann said, 'It's like abolishing apartheid, people want it to happen.'

Guardian, 3 June 2000, Michael Edmands interview.

The problems to overcome Seven million children die each year as a result of the debt crisis. Long-term economic and political causes of Africa's poverty and instability. Political instability, refusal by western finance to do a debt relief deal.

The method Public events like the human chain of 70,000 people at the Birmingham 1998 G8 conference. (The largest demonstration since Live Aid.)

The key steps Gaining commitment from President Clinton to cancel 100 per cent of the debt of the poorest countries. Public events and lobbying at July 2000 Okinawa G7 summit.

The learning that you can apply

- Go for the causes, not the symptoms of the problem.

- Form a coalition to create wider support for your cause.

- Find the big events in your organization. What are the big decision-making events in your firm? How do you get what you want on the agenda or lobby for the issues you believe are worthwhile?

Greenham Common Women's Peace Camp: protesting against cruise missiles

The objective To draw attention to the siting of tomahawk cruise missiles at US and RAF military bases in the UK, in order to prevent the installation of missiles in the UK. Greenham was the first location.

The team A wide assortment of women from all over the world. The founders, housewives from Wales and their families. A decision not to let men stay at the camp followed a series of events in which violence erupted following police intervention.

The values Everyone is welcome, we have no leaders, we are peaceful. Typified by song sung during actions – 'You can't kill the spirit, it is like a mountain, old and strong, it goes on and on' (Naomi Littlebear-Morena).

The wider stakeholders There was already an anti-nuclear campaign in place – CND, the Campaign for Nuclear Disarmament. And although the aims were the same, there was some tension between the more established CND hierarchy and Greenham Commoners. There was support from church groups, notably Quakers. The Labour Party gave support, although was at times bemused by the passion and heat of the campaign. There was huge international support from Japan – especially families of victims of the nuclear attacks on Hiroshima and Nagasaki, and from neutral countries such as Sweden and Switzerland.

The problems to overcome   A decision had been made to situate the missile by the highest level of NATO. It was in the context of US/USSR nuclear tension – Reagan and Thatcher railing against 'the evil empire'. Ordinary people were told that mutually assured destruction was the only way to maintain peace. There was no democratic process to decide the issue – it was ruled out. Also a number of people felt that we were Soviet supporters in trying to stop the missiles being installed.

The campaign method   Keeping a peaceful vigil outside the gates of the military base, plus co-ordinated non-violent direct action such as getting 10 000 women from all over the UK to hold hands around the perimeter fence (December 1982).

The media role   The media were split in their support. For the action above, the *Daily Mirror* (a popular tabloid) printed a special issue – full of praise for the brave ladies. Other reporters – notably from more right-of-centre political positions – depicted the Peace Camp as an anarchist ruse. We learned to give the media a good story and, above all, not to allow the media to find a leader. Whenever they said: 'Who is in charge here, love'? we said: 'I am. Can I help?' or sometimes: 'No one is.' Sometimes an unknown called Miss L Stopper became our leader. They usually asked us to lead us to her. Which was fun. Think about it.

The key steps Saying that everyone had personal responsibility for what happened at the Camp, everyone had a contribution – from making porridge in the morning on the camp fire to putting down a First Day Motion in the House of Commons. Gaining popular support, being very organized in logistics in the actions, encouraging a spirit of support and trust among those taking action.

The skills Determination to succeed, openness towards everyone who could contribute.

The outcome   Well, thanks to the protest, the United States does not have a nuclear missile site located 40 miles west of London. The UK government bowed to popular demand in 1985 and, although a number of cruise missiles were brought in, they were withdrawn over a two-year period. In 1998 the base was decommissioned. In March 2000 the local Berkshire council declared Greenham Common common heathland, with full public access and even a visitors centre. Plans are being made for a monument to mark the efforts of the Peace Camp women. In September 2000 the base protest finally came to an emotional end after 19 years of continuous protest.

The learning that you can apply:

- building a broad coalition
- developing a strategy for what you want to achieve
- using the media.

Persistence pays.

The Grameen Bank: microlending for profit Bangladesh

The objective Grameen-Banking caters for the poor. Grameen Bank provides credit to the poorest of the poor in rural

Bangladesh without any collateral. At Grameen Bank, credit is a cost-effective weapon to fight poverty and it serves as a catalyst in the overall development of socio-economic improvement.

The wider stakeholders Grameen family   There are more than a dozen organizations within the Grameen family of enterprises. These include the replication and research activities of Grameen Trust, handloom enterprises of Grameen Uddog/Handloom and fisheries pond management by Grameen Motsho/Fisheries Foundation.

The method   'We started giving out tiny loans under a system which later became known as the Grameen Bank, we never imagined that one day we would be reaching hundreds of thousands, let alone two million, borrowers.'

Microcredit is the extension of small loans to enterpreneurs too poor to qualify for traditional bank loans. It has proven an effective and popular measure in the ongoing struggle against poverty.

Common purpose
Uniting community need with private sector skills

Interview – Julia Middleton, Founder, Common Purpose

Common Purpose integrates private sector skills with public sector needs. In its ten-year history over 10,000 people have been through the Common Purpose training programme.

JM Julia Middleton
CM Carmel McConnell

CM *Julia, tell me about why you are an activist.*

JM I really hate squandering talent – I love the concept of people realizing that they are more than they have been told. And particularly in this country people are told that they won't amount to much. That wearing down – particularly of women – means that people don't believe that action is possible. I have people here who say, oh I can't do budgets, because someone at school told them they were no good at maths – I say get over it – learn it if it's going to be useful!

Also – I don't have barriers – at home I was not taught respect for my elders, the rich or kings. I was taught to respect talent. I have a talent and I have had the luck to be able to make a difference; I walked into the Industrial Society and was lucky enough to find a mentor – John Garnett – who taught me a great deal.

By my own values it would be wrong for me to squander the talents I have got.

I have no concept of the things I cannot do.

And I want to win. Not at sports, no – but through sheer bloodymindedness I get what I want. For example, we met with a potential sponsor and there was a lot of money at stake. The meeting went pear-shaped and at 5.00 there was no deal and that was it. That night I phoned every single person in the meeting and said I am not going to give up on this. And eventually we got the funding.

CM *What skills do you feel you have that have enabled you to be so successful?*

JM I am able to **produce clarity** – when others think things are confusing I am able to see clearly and find a way through. That is important – because figuring out how to do things, how to get people to really work together, is complex.

I have a lot of **physical stamina** – you really need to be able to see it through. When you are tired you can't inspire.

You have to have some **management skills** – I always tell people to learn their leadership skills when they are young – and I delegate a lot. I think everyone makes mistakes when learning – the earlier you can learn from mistakes in your career the better. The Industrial Society made me a leader.

Communication – written and oral. I can produce a fantastic one-page overview. I can't write two pages! I remember someone asking a little girl, what are you trying to say? The right question is 'What do you want the other person to understand?' There's a big difference.

Be able to make a great speech. Watch brilliant speeches – find a way to make lots of them.

I listen to the Winston Churchill and Martin Luther King tapes – and they are fantastic. Get the audience to really listen and repeat the message – keep on saying it because people often don't get it the first few times.

Learn to do detail. Learn the budget back to front, be on top of the material – you need to.

Reinvent yourself – I came back from each one of my five pregnancies with a completely different outlook on where we needed to go. The markets change constantly and if you are a chief executive and you want the company to grow you have to reinvent yourself to simply keep up. I have constantly asked people for help – on deal-making, on company strategy – and made myself find people who would be able to give me the best possible understanding. People do want to help.

Care enough about people to tell the truth – even if it risks your popularity.

Feel responsible for people around you – what about the people who live in your street? Are they happy, working? Can you give them a job? I have done that – being an activist means thinking about the people in your street.

CM *Do you take care of yourself?*

JM I never ever work at weekends and I am tremendously lucky to have a home life that gives me loads of happiness. I maybe should exercise more but prefer to see my kids and I don't think it would be possible to do this job on less hours. But on a Friday night we go to our home in Wiltshire and the kids and my husband have my undivided attention, and we have a great time together. I feel incredibly lucky to have the life I have.

Jubilee 2000, Greenham Common, Grameen Bank and Common Purpose. Social activism; ordinary people creating extraordinary change. What might be the lesson for you, right now?

Mother Teresa said: 'We cannot do great things. We can only do small things with great love.' And my belief is that a coalition of people doing small things with great love, together, really can change the world.

There is no hierarchy of oppression – or contribution

One characteristic of the recent anti-capitalism campaigns – in my view– has been the creation of business as arch enemy. The assessment that all people in business are bad. But isn't business an amoral concept? Money is neither good nor bad. It's just an exchange mechanism. Social exclusion is bad. Racism that believes that one country has superiority over another is bad. But trade in itself isn't always the baddie. Trade can exploit the weaker party. And often does. Trade also pays the taxes that keep our social welfare system intact. Business creates the opportunity for infrastructure development that simply wouldn't exist if charity were the only sponsor. The trade not aid agenda recognizes that we all want to make our own independent way in the world. Not just charity. So let us try to disentangle the 'business bad, protest good' arguments with some analysis of what really goes on. Before we create more separation.

The mindset that some people are better than others has been the cause of so much human pain and suffering. The racism of the 'white man's burden' decimated African culture. The catholic conquistadors depriving our world of the manifold intellectual gains of Aztec and Mayan culture in Central and Latin America. We still haven't changed a worldwide scam, which means women do most of the world's work and earn a fraction of the world's income.

I hate and detest the damage being done to our environment for profit. But I wouldn't put myself up as judge of anyone else – I would hope that the people making decisions haven't yet realized they don't need to cheat, pollute or destroy the planet in order to win financially. Profit does not have to mean punishing the earth. There is a huge challenge here – to educate ourselves in the intellectual redistribution of wealth. More food than can be eaten is produced every year. It just doesn't get spread very evenly. To understate.

Perhaps this certainty about friend and foe is a function of age. When I was 21 things definitely seemed clearer. 'We had to fight the nukes – it was the most important thing in the world.' Then, with campaigner Laura Nickerson, I spent a year talking to over 500 groups all over the USA, talking about European resistance to nuclear missiles and tracing the lifecycle of uranium through the nuclear development process. Being in those different communities changed my mind. There I was, a young white woman being supported by public donations to put forward a dissenting viewpoint to the establishment. I began to realize how fortunate I was, meeting people for whom it would be nice to worry only about nuclear war. They had to worry about having enough food to eat and fresh water to drink – so

But despite those injustices, it seems naïve to polarize debate to the level where all environmentalists are good; all those engaged in business are bad. This has happened in some parts of the protest movements. It seems to me that there is a choice about the level of contribution we all have to give – and that it doesn't require any person to become an enemy.

dealing with the threat of global nuclear annihilation was some way down their day-to-day list of priorities. Talking to refugees from El Salvador and Nicaragua. Spending time understanding the history of American Indian people as they opposed uranium mining on their sacred ancestral land.

So I became less sure, over time, about quite who is friend and foe. And I have decided to expect that everyone would want to do the good thing given the opportunity. This attitude has served me well and I am grateful for the many times that it has been re-inforced. And in the same way, it seems sensible to value all kinds of contribution to improving the world.

One of the changes I hope will come is a recognition that everyone has a contribution to make. Let us look at the problems to be solved and solve them without having to make more difference in the world.

Finally. In praise of what you do . . . next

Personal change is happening to you right now. As a result of what happened today you have more or less choice about what happens to you tomorrow. That's it. We plan to change. From being controlled to being more in control of our lives. So we're all involved in change. See yourself as a personal activist. Get passionate about your own choices and I'm confident you'll become more powerful. Compound that change of people getting seriously excited about personally living to thine own self be true. Imagine everyone you know getting stronger, clearer on their life's work. Maybe a world of less fear. Maybe a world where we become more respectful of our natural diversity as human beings. Even – if I can squeeze one last drop from the Darwin analogy – using our economic and social diversity as a successful component of species survival.

Fascism becomes extinct in the natural world. Diversity flourishes. Free trade is a good thing. We need to create and move capital to develop our infrastructures, our new technologies. But without checks and balances free trade increases the causes of poverty and pollution and destroys endless numbers of precious human spirits in the cause of market growth and share price.

The good news is that we have here a force for balance. We have you and me and thousands of other change activists. If we are able to help each other, free trade as the single most dominant world order will evolve and thrive afresh as a new hybrid. A force for profit and social improvement.

It won't be overnight and as with all change, there will be the occasional moments of confusion. I believe this change connection between trade and activists will – like broadband connectivity – bring new heart and soul to the global marketplace. The broadband connected planet brought to it by you and me, the change activists. Globally networked protesters is one phrase I keep seeing. People who live close to their heart I call it.

Who'd have thought it. Dear reader, by taking action to help business see the whole picture, we may well be saving the planet.

So the big opportunity we have now is to take action in our lives, each one of us, to live out this broader and more compassionate perspective. To create, in the words of John Bird, a strengthened bottom line, including action to address social issues.

The change activist is a hybrid, capable of business success, able to understand and steer their career by action on personal values. Lives by Activist Rule 1 *to thine own self be true*. Insists on working with a sense of social contribution as a way of finding their true path.

The change activist integrates hitting the strengthened bottom line into the job description, team goal and finally into company objectives. Really. That way we can all help world trade solve humanities problems. Without risking lower profit. In fact as the following article shows, probably creating more.

'Business has a vital interest in understanding the values and goals of the critics of globalisation for two reasons. First, pressure groups articulate and shape the public mind more pervasively and effectively than any political party and they have a leverage on events that is often greater than that of government. If business ignores these realities it will pay a big price.'

John Gray, Professor of European Thought,
London School of Economics, *Financial Times*, 31 October 2000

If I can help

The only way to do it,   If I can help, let me know. I am
is to do it.   carmelmcconnell@hotmail.com
                              and my commitment is to stay true
to my change activist and make things happen. And help you
become better acquainted with your own.

This is your journey.

References
In the spirit of contribution here is a web page that will link
you to a taster of useful and caring sites. The site has reading
lists and other useful information. Check it out.
www.yourmomentum.com/changeactivist/links

Links to:
www.changeactivist.com
www.magicsandwich.co.uk
www.corpwatch.org
www.hungersite.com
www.commonpurpose.org.uk
www.dropthedebt.org
www.grameen.org
www.greenpeace.org
www.rainforestconcern.org
www.acas.org.uk
www.citizensconnection.net

Public seminars and courses
A series of one-hour practical seminars to explore the ideas in
Change Activist are available.

The author runs a leadership programme based on the ideas in *Change Activist* and *Soultrader* (Momentum, 2002). For more information, see www.changeactivist.com or contact carmelmcconnell@hotmail.com

Thank you.

Other books by Carmel McConnell:

Soultrader

find purpose and you'll find success

1 84304018 2

You're a busy, stressed employee. Your job is probably pretty much ok; maybe better, maybe worse. But whichever, you probably don't have much time or energy to devote to thinking about anything much, outside of coping with workload and what to have for dinner. What difference would it make to your life if you were creating the 'lifelong adventure called my career' based on who you are – at core?

How would you like to feel excited about your life again? Because that's what soultrading is all about. Your soul can help you figure out what you want to be when you grow up. Much more than the boss ever could.

And how would you like to be more successful and high-achieving? Because that's also what soultrading is about – having a personal strategy that you really buy into (and so do others). Discover the 12-day *Soultrader* plan to work out your purpose and develop your personal strategy.

Careers un-ltd

tell me. what is it you plan to do with your one wild and precious life?

Carmel McConnell and Jonathan Robinson
1 84304026 3

You can choose if you want a limited career, or an un-ltd one. This is a very different kind of career book. It's the first ever guide to explore ALL your career options – not just life in big corporates – for anybody who wants more from their career than just a pay packet. It's the rough guide to the world of work. Featuring the profiles of 10 career pioneers who tell how they created an un-ltd career for themselves, *Careers Un-ltd* will help you think through what you want to do with YOUR 'wild and precious' life.

Available at all good bookshops and online at:
www.business-minds.com   www.yourmomentum.com

Change Activism Where You Work

If you liked the ideas in this book, a number of workplace or personal change seminars are available based around the ideas in *Change Activist* and *Soultrader*. A brave alternative to the same old, same old.

See **changeactivist.com** for more details, or call 0207 485 7681.

The Purposeful Leader Programme

A two-day programme based on *Change Activist* and *Soultrader*. Learn
- what you really want to be when you grow up
- how to identify the fears that might be holding you back — and how to get over it
- building a trust based workplace
- social activism in your own life (media management, focus, action orientation)
- the benefits waiting when your business becomes a socially responsible business
- what makes you happy — and how to create a career based on what you really want
- feeling in control, for beginners.

Available for groups of 6–16 with individual coaching options.

Rapid Results Workshops

Two-hour facilitated event. Make big things happen fast.
Solve the problem — don't agonise act!
Can be scary. Is very effective. Not recommended for fossils.

Available for groups of 2–30

Lets Do Diversity (properly)

A half day seminar to look at the hot topic of workplace diversity and inclusion. With the change activist, without the PC guilt, business number watching or old boys club mindset. Do you want a feedback rich, genuinely trust-based workplace? This seminar gets everyone involved in that process. Expect a genuine challenge to your workplace norms.

Available for groups of 2–200

Change Activist Coaching

A professional development coach (and activist) will spend two half-day sessions with you, to help you figure out
- your career options
- your motivation
- what kind of activist might be hiding in there
- what kind of action you need to take
- with lots of handholding as you make big things happen fast.

Available to anyone who really wants to change. A nightmare if you don't.

The Magic Sandwich

The Magic Sandwich is a child poverty initiative, started by *Change Activist* author Carmel McConnell in May 2000.

Carmel was appalled to learn that many UK children go to school without breakfast and cannot learn because of hunger. She found that primary school teachers regularly had to bring in fruit from their own pocket, to help children in their classrooms.

After consultation with a number of headteachers in the London Borough of Hackney a pilot project was set up with five schools in the borough, to supply breakfast food to the children. This trial has been running successfully since September 2001, with more schools joining the scheme in September 2002. The plan is to extend food delivery and nutrition awareness into other parts of the country in 2003. Teachers report a range of benefits from Magic Sandwich support – most often that children are more settled and able to learn at the start of the school day. Your purchase of this book means that roughly 65p will go to the Magic Sandwich charity – so thank you.

Aims and Objectives:

- The Magic Sandwich aims to provide nutritious food to school children at risk of malnutrition and to raise nutrition awareness.
- To educate children, their parents and schools staff on the link between nutrition, academic performance, health and general well-being.
- To improve the learning ability of children with better nutrition.
- To raise the awareness of the effects of poor nutrition with children, their parents and school staff and to offer advice and support.
- To improve and supplement the diet of schoolchildren.
- To involve professionals from large companies to take an interest in the children and their diet, become socially aware and gain 'hands on' experience within a structured, professionally mentored development programme the profits from which will be covenanted to the Magic Sandwich.

The project welcomes input from anyone interested in supporting the academic success of primary schoolchildren. We run regular seminars involving parents, teachers, nutritionists and local business leaders. For more information on how to get involved, please contact:

The Magic Sandwich, 5b Belmont Street, London NW1 8HJ

See **www.magicsandwich.co.uk** for more information.

If you want to contribute financially to our work, we welcome cheques made payable to the Magic Sandwich to the same address. Thanks again.

Magic Outcomes – development that makes a difference

Are you a change activist?
Would you like a little help to get there?

Magic Outcomes is a leadership development programme that really makes a difference. How? Because all profits from the Magic Outcomes programme goes to support primary schools, buying food and providing nutrition awareness. This is critical, because for 1 in 4 UK children the only hot food received is at school. (Child Poverty Action Group).

How does it work?

Magic Outcomes provides skill development in a social leadership context: participants work in a professional 'change activist' context in the schools community. Typically the Magic Outcomes student spends 1 day per month on a practical, schools-based project. This is challenging. For example, how do you build trust with diverse stakeholders? Could you produce a business case for change where you work? Do you care enough about your development to go outside your comfort zone? The programme helps you do all that. And if you can be credible and trustworthy with primary school children, hard pressed teachers and parents – you can build trust with any customer anywhere.

There is real potential for joint problem solving between your organisation and the community. High performance requires leaders with both social and business vision, Magic Outcomes delivers that, and at the same time addresses child poverty.

Change Activist Training

Excellent development support is provided throughout the programme. This includes:

- Structured workshops to provide skills and knowledge development in key areas (valuing diversity, consumer trends, project leadership, gaining action muscle).
- One-to-one mentoring (with experienced public and private sector mentors).
- Knowledge to help you understand how the public and voluntary sector operates.
- Help to explore a range of socially fulfilling career options.
- Business measures to ensure skills are transferred back to the workplace.

If you would like to gain leadership skills, and make a difference, get in touch at **info@magicsandwich.co.uk** or call 0207 485 7681.

This is how to create leadership skills and social responsibility in the same programme. We'd love to get your change activism into action.

momentum prescription – Let Us Help You Work Out Which Book Will Suit Your Symptoms

Feel stuck in a rut? Something wrong and need help doing something about it?

◆ If you need tools to help making changes in your life: **coach yourself** (a good general guide to change)

◆ If you are considering dramatic career change: **snap, crackle or stop**

◆ If you need to work out what you'd like to be doing and how to get there: **be your own career consultant**

◆ If you need help making things happen and tackling the 'system' at work/in life: **change activist**

Feel that you can never make decisions and you just let things 'happen'?

◆ If you need help making choices: **the big difference**

◆ If you want to feel empowered and start making things happen for yourself: **change activist**

Feel life is too complicated and overwhelming?

◆ If you need help working through office politics and complexity: **clued up**

◆ If you need a kick up the backside to get out of your commerce-induced coma: **change activist**

◆ If you need an amusing and very helpful modern life survival guide: **innervation**

◆ If you never have enough time or energy to get things done or think properly: **mental space**

Feel like you might be in the wrong job?

◆ If you want help finding your destiny job and inspiration to make that dramatic career change: **snap, crackle or stop**

◆ If you feel like you aren't doing a job that is really what you are about': **soultrader**

◆ If you are struggling with the 'do something worthwhile OR make money dilemma': **change activist**